C000177021

The Story of Kemsing in Kent

ISBN 0 - 9504703 - 2 - 5
Published by Kemsing Historical and Art Society and Kemsing Parish Council
Printed by The Caxton & Holmesdale Press, Sevenoaks, Kent
Design & Typesetting by Computer Techniques, Kemsing, Kent

THE STORY OF KEMSING IN KENT

V. E. BOWDEN

1994

*'For the people of Kemsing,
present and to come'*

CONTENTS

Author's Note

I have called this book the Story of Kemsing because it is by no means a thoroughly researched history, as I am not a trained historian. I have merely "collected" material from any source that has come my way during the past fifty years. I am, therefore, indebted to a number of people whose books and notes I have been able to read, some of which are listed at the back. Looking back through a large number of as yet unclassified notes I realise that a great deal of information has failed to be included, but I hope that one day a qualified person will take on the task of writing a real "History of Kemsing". For the mistakes, mis-statements and other errors I am sure to have made I apologise, and I hope that erudite readers will put me right where necessary.

Acknowledgement

The author wishes to thank the following Kemsing residents for the work and contributions they have made in the production of this book,

His wife and son Mark - Editing and Diagrams
Rosemary Banister - Typing
Frank White - Photography
Allen Bryant - Project Management
Jim Panks - Layout & Typesetting
Kemsing Historical and Art Society

Foreword

Shortly after the founding of the Kemsing Historical and Art Society, (KHAS), Vic told me of a chronology of the village which he had been compiling over the years, going back to the beginning of time (almost) to the present. It was, however, in bits and pieces and here and there, really only the bare bones of an outline: but, for reference work he thought it would be nice to have a fair copy and keep it in the Library for all to use. I duly typed the chronology and learnt so much about the village I had come to live in. What a fund of knowledge, of magic, myth and reality, this man had in his head! And having worked from those bits and pieces, it was indeed good to know that the chronology was collated, albeit in sketch form.

It was the Clerk of the Parish Council, Rosemary Banister, who had the wit to draw the elements together. She persuaded Vic that the time had come to make that extra effort and put flesh on the bones of a jolly good story, that of Kemsing in Kent. Between us, the KHAS and the Parish Council nurtured Vic and Rosemary in their endeavours and Vic nursed his story and we have the result here in this volume.

The KHAS is enormously proud to have Vic as its founding President, for in so many ways he is Mr. Kemsing himself. He epitomises all that is best in a village historian, and we are delighted that this publication has come about well within his lifetime.

Melinda Robinson
Chairman, KHAS

Kemsing Village

Extract from Samuel Bagshaw's Directory of Kent 1847.

"Kemsing parish and village, 3½ miles N.E. from Sevenoaks, is situated at the foot of the chalk hills. Near the centre of the village is St. Edith's well, a famous saint said to have been born here, and to have wrought many miracles ..... The church is dedicated to St. Edith."

Chapter 1
Early Years

Romans & Saxons

The name Kemsing is apparently a Saxon one, although even the experts are not sure what it means. It was once spelt CIMESCING, which was thought at one time to mean the place or clan of a man called CYME, because the suffix "ing" usually means "the family or home of ". This, however, has been questioned, and some say it is merely a word meaning "the beautiful place" or "the King's fortress". Recent research suggests another possibility; in other parts of southern England it has been found that, in a few cases, names ending in "-ing" were originally the names of small streams. It is at least a possibility, therefore, that Kemsing was the early name of the stream which rises in the centre of the village. Throughout the centuries the spelling has varied to include Cimisinga, Camesing, Kemsynge, and Kempsing.

However, we know that people were in this district long before the Saxons arrived. Prehistoric finds in Kemsing have been meagre, consisting of only a few worked flints found in ploughed fields from time to time, but prehistoric sites in neighbouring parishes show that the area was extensively occupied from the Palaeolithic period right through to the late Iron Age. In the Roman period the evidence becomes stronger. The Darent may have been a more considerable river then, and it has been suggested that it was used for the transport of grain in barges. The well-known villa at Lullingstone was not only the centre of a large agricultural estate, but is also thought to have been a collecting and re-distribution centre for grain grown in the Darent valley and Holmesdale.

There were villas at Otford and Ightham, both neighbouring parishes, but in Kemsing itself, the only indication of a Roman site on the Ordnance Survey maps was at Springhead, which is now covered by the houses in Brookfield and Oxenhill Road. It has not been identified, but is thought to have been either a grain-drying plant or a water mill; either interpretation would support the notion that corn-growing was a significant element in the economy of the area. Some amateur archaeological work was done on the site in the 1950s and several artefacts and coins were sent to the British Museum. Scattered pieces of tessellated paving and some pieces of brooches and pins have been found in Oxenhill Road, and also a coin in Montfort Road.The latter, dating to about AD 318, was minted during the reign of the Emperor Constantus at Trier on the River Moselle.

In the mid 20th century, the remains consisted of a rectangular chamber with walls of two or three feet high, which served as a playground for local children.

Apart from this, some few potsherds and tiles of Roman date were unearthed near to Childsbridge in Childsbridge Lane when the railway was built in 1874, and the claypit which was behind the railway station and is now part of the Chaucer Business Park is thought to have been a source for the material for the making of Roman bricks and tiles, though no evidence to support this idea has yet been found.

What happened here between the dispersal of the Roman culture in England from AD 410 and the first mention of Kemsing in a document in AD 822, is not clear. Undoubtedly, when the Saxons and Jutes arrived in Kent, either as invaders or foederati *(mercenary soldiers in Roman pay)* and moved up the river valleys to make settlements, one such party would have found what was essential to a settlement, namely water, here at Kemsing, where the springline between the chalk downs and the clay valley is very obvious. So, perhaps, in the fifth and sixth centuries, a development grew up around what is now known as St. Edith's Well.

As Christianity spread through Kent from about AD 600, it is probable that a church was built to serve this little community on the site of the present church. There is in the churchyard to-day the remains of an old yew tree, which has been reckoned by David Bellamy and his advisers to be 1300 years old. This may have been the meeting point for pagan ceremonies as were practised by the immigrant Saxons. Such sites were often converted for Christian use by the missionaries, and that was therefore a suitable place for a church.

In 1880 two skeletons were found in a field about 750 yards to the west of Kemsing church, possibly about where Highfield Road is now. One of them was accompanied by a spearhead, a common grave-furnishing in the early Anglo-Saxon period. These should therefore be pagan burials but it seems that early converts to Christianity in Kent were reluctant to abandon the practice of placing personal goods in the graves of the dead, so these two burials may be of Christians, or nominal Christians, rather than pagans. They cannot be later than the first quarter of the eighth century, however, when the practice finally ceased. No proper archaeological record was made and the skeletons were re-buried in the churchyard by the Revd. G. Bridges Lewis, on the boundary to the north of the choir door.

Some of the area would have been heavily wooded, and the Saxons used the woods for rearing pigs to serve the small settlements like Kemsing and Wrotham. Possibly Heverham came into being as a clearing in which the swineherds lived.

Until recently, this place name was spelt Everham, and the derivation is perhaps from the Old English "eofor", the place of boars.

To the north of the settlements of Kemsing and Heverham ran a track now known as the Pilgrims Way, thought to be one of the oldest used tracks in the country, connecting the West with the outlets to the continent on the Kent Coast. As Kent was, during the sixth and seventh centuries, a paramount kingdom maintaining strong contacts both with the rest of England and with southern Scandinavia and northern France, such routeways were of considerable significance.

It was not until AD 822 that definite mention is made of an area called Kemsing. This occurs in a document which describes the acquisition by Wulfred, Archbishop of Canterbury, from Ceolwulf, King of the Mercians, of a parcel of land which constituted what became the Manor of Kemsing. It is described as "West and North Greotan edisces land: east Cymiescinas cert: South Andred". It included what are now Kemsing, Seal, Godden Green and Underriver.

This was a much larger tract of country than is represented by the present Parish of Kemsing. Wulfred was much concerned to increase the holding of the Church in land throughout his archdiocese, and it is probable that he paid for this and that it was not just a grant from the King.

When Ceolwulf died in 825, there was a danger that Wulfred would lose this land, and possibly other areas, because they were claimed by a female member of Ceolwulf's family. However, he attended a Witenagemot *(a gathering of counsellors)* called by Ceolwulf's successor, Beornwulf, and succeeded in obtaining the surrender of these estates to himself.

ST. EDITH

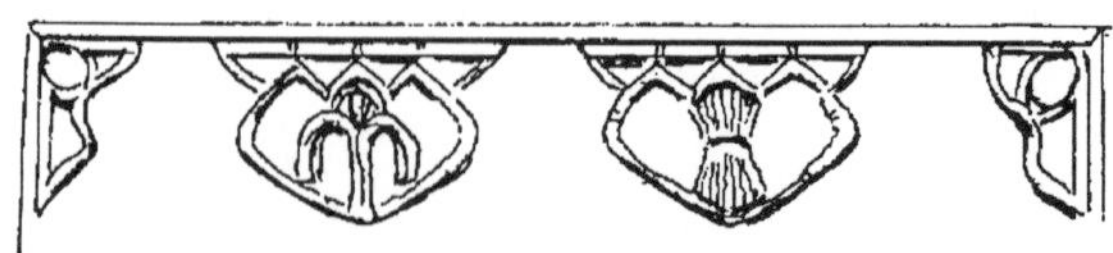

A great deal has been written about the life and times of St. Edith of Wilton. Here we can only include a summary of these writings.

In the year AD 961, the King of England was Edgar, a great-grandson of King Alfred the Great. He succeeded his brother Edwy, and inherited a kingdom made up of seven or eight petty kingdoms, whose rulers eventually recognised him as the King of all

England. During his reign no further wars were waged, and he earned the nickname of "Edgar the Peaceful". His adviser was Dunstan, Archbishop of Canterbury, and a leading Benedictine, who was a tower of strength to the throne.

GENEALOGICAL TABLE

showing the descendants of Alfred the Great, from whom St. Edith derives her origin

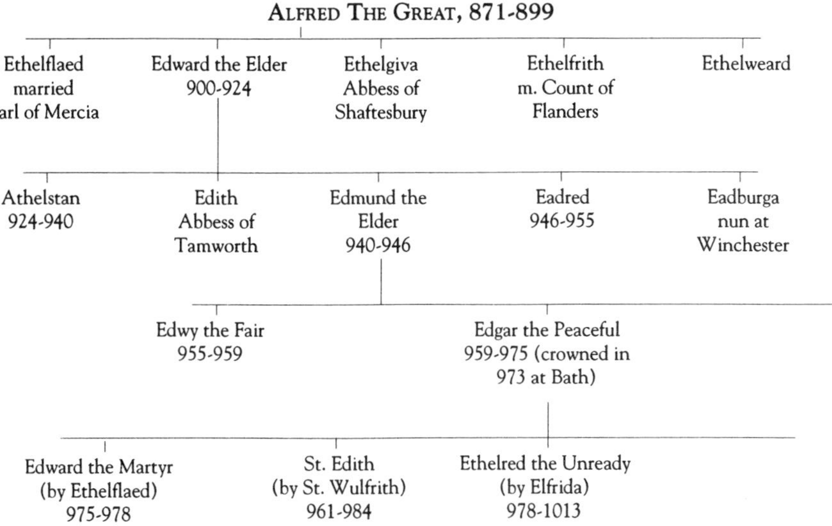

While visiting Wilton Abbey on one occasion, Edgar made the acquaintance of a young lady called Wulfrith, who was residing at the Abbey because her father, a noble called Godwin, had died, and she was being educated there. Edgar took Wulfrith, perhaps by handfast marriage, and brought her to a house in Otford.

In due course, when she was expecting a child, he took her to a small convent in Kemsing, which is thought to have been on the site of the present Box House. There, the baby Edith was born in the year generally reckoned AD 961, but sometimes reported as 962. This discrepancy may be accounted for by the fact that in those days the year began on 25th March, not 1st January as it does today.

Whether Wulfrith took advantage of the custom whereby partners to a handfast marriage could part after a year, or whether there had been no marriage, is not certain, but Wulfrith returned to Wilton with the child when the latter was quite small. Edgar always regarded his daughter as a member of the Royal House, and treated her as a Princess. He was present when she was professed as a nun, at the age of fourteen. The strictness of the Benedictine order had yet to be applied to the nuns, and Edith, perhaps inheriting something of the gaiety and splendour of her father, delighted to dress occasionally in the finest clothes and jewellery. When rebuked by Bishop Athelwold of Winchester, Edith took in his somewhat shabby appearance and said, "pride could lurk even in rags".

Her brother Edward, who had succeeded their father to the throne in AD 975, was murdered at Corfe Castle, Dorset, at the instigation of his stepmother Elfrida.

The nobles were not willing to have another half-brother Ethelred, as King, and they offered the crown to Edith. By that time, however, she was committed to the life of a nun, and she refused the crown. She later became Abbess of Wilton, where her life was one of holiness and devotion. Towards the end of her life, she founded a church near the abbey, dedicated to St. Denis. At the dedication service, St. Dunstan was so impressed by her devoutness that he prophesied that she would die soon, and that the thumb with which she crossed herself would not see corruption.

Probably due to the selfless way in which she devoted her time and energy to serving others, even in adverse circumstances, she died at the early age of 23, on September 16th AD 984, only six weeks after St. Dunstan's prophecy.

Persistent rumours that miracles were wrought at her tomb caused King Canute many years later to have it opened, for he could not believe that any child of Edgar could be a saint. Nevertheless, he found her body incorrupt, and was so impressed at this relevation that he caused an ornate shrine to be erected over her grave.

There were several saints in the Saxon Royal family. St. Edith's great-aunt, another Edith, was called St. Edith of Tamworth. Her half-brother Edward, murdered at Corfe Castle, became St Edward the Martyr, and a nephew, who succeeded to the throne of England in 1042, is known to history as St. Edward the Confessor. Her mother, Wulfrith, whose name has been spelt as Wulfrida, Wilfreda, Wulfride and Welfhide, was also venerated as a saint.

Many different accounts of Wulfrith's meeting with King Edgar appeared throughout the ages, mostly of a romantic nature.

According to one story, the King, finding that she did not want to leave the abbey, arranged with her kinswoman called Wenfleda, to coax her out of the Abbey by a subterfuge. She pretended to be ill and dying, and sent word to Wilton that she wanted to see Wulfrith before she died. When Wulfrith arrived at her house, she found Edgar waiting for her. Wenfleda put royal apparel on the girl and sat her beside the King, who invited guests to attend his wedding. But Wulfrith wept and escaped to her own chamber and set guard at her door. She left by a window and made her way back to Wilton. Edgar pursued her and eventually carried her off.

After the birth of St. Edith at Kemsing, Wulfrith returned to Wilton and took the veil in about AD 963, and eventually became an Abbess.

In AD 969 she was present, with her daughter, at the translation of the body of St. Edward the Martyr, and she is also said to have attended the service in 987 at which St. Edith was canonised, although there appears to be no historic record of such an event. It is likely that Edith was accorded her title and status of saint by the people of the day out of respect for her devotion and holiness of life.

Some thirty years after her death St. Edith's nephew, King Edmund Ironside, defeated the Danes, under their leader Canute, at the battle of Otford in AD 1016. Kemsing people may have seen some of the fighting that took place. It has sometimes been conjectured that the two skeletons found in 1880 *(mentioned above)* were victims of this battle but they cannot be of such a late date; they are probably normal burials of the early Saxon period.

Reports that men ploughing the hundred acre field between Kemsing and Otford in the early twentieth century sometimes unearthed fragments of metal that could have been weapons gave rise to a suggestion that this area was the site of a Saxon burial ground. Again, there is no official confirmation for this, and iron-work rarely survives in ploughsoil for so long; any such finds are probably pieces of relatively recent agricultural equipment.

THE NORMANS

Although the church and parish must have been well established by the time of the making of the Domesday book in 1086, there is no mention of Kemsing in it. However, it does mention Seal *(La Sela)*, which probably covered the parish of Kemsing. The reference reads, "Geoffrey de Ros holds of Bishop Odo *(William the Conqueror's brother)* La Sela; 7 sulongs, 3 ploughs, 31 villeins, 14 bordars with 16 ploughs, 9 slaves. Fishing yielding 90 eels. Woodland. 75 swine. Manor worth 40 pounds in King Edward's time, £16 now. Brixi Cilt held it of King Edward".

The fifty-four people mentioned here would have had wives and families, so there may have been as many as two or three hundred people scattered round the parish. But where was the fishing that yielded ninety eels? Possibly in the Guzzle Brook, or in the stew pond that once was fed by the brook on its north side where it ran under Childsbridge Lane. But who was Brixi Cilt, and where did he live?

The Church of St. Mary the Virgin was built in the second half of the eleventh century, probably about the year AD 1060. It consisted of a nave and possibly a small semi-circular sanctuary.

The existing south wall is regarded as the only part of the original remaining and, as this is built of rubble on very shallow foundations, it is considered that the rest was built in a similar manner, with walls thicker at the base than at the top to give strength to support the roof. These walls are not so thick as in most Saxon churches. However, the opening in the south side was of the high-arched type that the Saxons used. The outline of this doorway can still be detected under the porch. The roof may have been of thatch, and there was possibly a small window in the sanctuary and another in the south wall.

The existence of the church is not recorded until the preparation of a document known as the Textus Roffensis round about AD 1115 to 1120. This listed all the churches and chapels in the diocese of Rochester which paid money for chrism oil to the cathedral authorities. In the case of Kemsing the amount paid was ninepence, which was the rate for a church as opposed to sixpence for a chapel. It is believed that this list was an updated version of an earlier one, made in Saxon times. If so, it shows that there was a church in Kemsing before the present building.

The Castle

In 1135 Henry I died and was succeeded by Stephen after a great deal of internal warfare between Stephen and his cousin Mathilda. Stephen, though brave and generous, lacked qualities of statesmanship, decision and firmness, and was surrounded by barons who were definitely warlike, and wished to be independent. There was so much trouble in the land that each was concerned to look to his own, and many of them were responsible for building castles on their own land as a precaution against attack by their neighbours. Many of these were built without Royal permission and they were known as "adulterine" castles. It is possible that Kemsing Castle was built at this time. The exact site is not known but it is assumed that it stood on the ground called "Castle Bank", which is the area of land now occupied by the houses and gardens of "Castle Bank" and "The Keep". The northern end of "The Keep" garden is an artifically raised mound at least four feet high, and the fact that this area was known in Elizabethan days as "Castle Bank" seems to indicate that this was indeed the site of the castle. If this location is correct the castle was a small earthwork of the type known by archaeologists as a "ring-work", probably surmounted by a timber palisade and containing a timber tower and buildings; hall, service rooms, stables, storehouses and so forth.

Water was available from the well, and some of the houses round about would have held people who served at the castle.

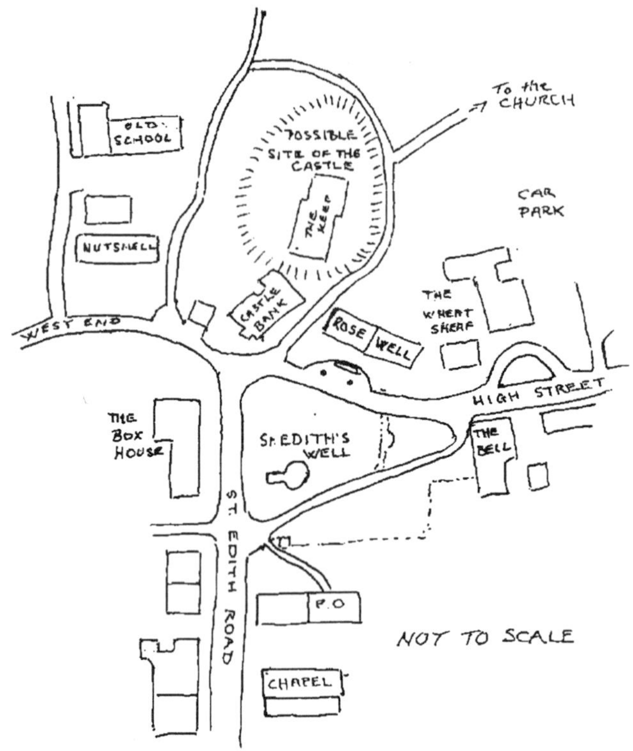

The occupants of the castle were usually sub-tenants, retainers, or bailiffs of the Lords of the Manor of Kemsing. Thomas Philipot, writing in 1659, said that in 1152, when King Stephen died and Henry II came to the throne, Kemsing Castle was "a place then of important Concernment, though now it's Skeleton itself be shrunk into such a desolate and neglected Masse of Rubbish, that it would be now as difficult to trace it out and find it, as it was formerly to conquer it."

Meanwhile, in the next parish of Ightham an important family had succeeded to the Yaldham Estate. This family, known as de Aldeham, held three main properties, Great Yaldham, Little Yaldham and West Yaldham. Sir Thomas de Aldeham served with Richard Coeur de Lion at the siege of Askelon, where he distinguished himself by some either noble or perhaps foolhardy deed which earned him the approval of King Richard, who knighted him on the field.

The de Aldeham family died out in 1290 when there were no more male members and the property was divided between two sisters, one of whom married Sir John de St. Clere, and thereafter their house was called Aldeham St Cleres. The other, Margery Peckham, inherited what is now Yaldham Manor.

With the beginning of the thirteenth century, changes were made in the building of the parish church. The small semi-circular apse which is believed to have occupied the east end of the church was demolished. The material taken from it was used to extend the south wall as a wall for a new chancel, which would be rectangular. As there was insufficient of this rubble material to continue the new building, stone had to be imported, possibly from the Maidstone area, for the east and north walls. This rectangular chancel was some three times the size of the original semi-circular apse. A little material was incorporated into the west end of the church in the form of a right-angled buttress.

Ye Aldeham - The Old Homestead

11th century: apsidal Sanctuary

Early 13th century: new Chancel and Sanctuary

Late 13th century: Nave extension

c.1340 the Wedding Porch

16th century: Turret and Spire

1878: a Vestry added

1891: north Aisle and vestries

1891: the west end

Stages in the building of the church of
St Mary - the - Virgin

Chapter 2
Medieval Kemsing

Countess Eleanor

The Lordship of the Manor had by now passed to William Marshall, Earl of Pembroke, who fell out of favour with King John *(1199 to 1216)*, and the manor was alienated to Fulk de Brent. Within a few years, however, William, Earl of Pembroke was reinstated. His son, William Marshall II, married the Princess Eleanor, King John's daughter, who thus became the Lady of the Manor of Kemsing. Her brother, who was by now on the throne as Henry III, was not pleased with this marriage, and made provision for the title of the Lordship of the Manor to revert to Eleanor if she outlived William Marshall.

This, in fact, she did, being only sixteen years old when, after three years of marriage, Pembroke died. Eleanor was determined not to marry again, and with a friend retired to the country, possibly to a manor house at Kemsing, where she was in residence off and on for some further eight years. In 1225, King Henry III issued an order to William the Carpenter, to take timber for making palings or fences from the park at Kemsing, which lay round or close to the Manor House, to Dover by water. How this was done is not clear.

There are further references to Countess Eleanor, as she was known throughout Henry III's reign. In 1232, he directed his soldiers and the free men of Kemsing to help the Countess to pay her debts. He also ordered the Sheriff of Kent to provide oak trees from Kemsing, Sutton, and Braborne Manors, to help in the repair of Dover Castle. The following year, he allowed to the Countess twenty oak trees from his land at Tonbridge, in order to repair her Manor House, which had been damaged by fire.

From these references we know that there was a house of some substance in the parish, and a park. The park is sometimes shown on later maps, but the whereabouts of the house is not known. Its fate is also unknown; possibly it was not maintained after the Countess's time, for it is not mentioned again in the records, though doubtless materials from the building were re-used elsewhere in the locality.

There is no doubt that Eleanor and later her husband, Simon de Montfort, whom she married in 1238, had the interest of the village at heart, for on the ninth of August 1233 the Countess obtained a grant from her brother, King Henry III, of a weekly market and an annual fair in the village on the vigil, day and morrow of St Edith *(the sixteenth of September)*. According to the charter roll No. 17 of Henry III, this fair was to be held near to her manor at Seal. From that, we can conjecture that the park and perhaps the manor house lay between the villages of Kemsing and Seal. Lanes called Park Lane in both villages probably led towards the manor house. In 1236, three men were found poaching in the park at Kemsing. One was called Andrew the Scot, who with Richard of Wareham, and Osbert Gendum, was engaged in a fight, during which one man was killed, and these three were held to answer a charge of murder, but the Countess Eleanor sued for their pardon.

Some years after her marriage to Simon de Montfort, King Henry III paid a visit to Otford Manor House, which stood in the vicinity of what was later known as Otford Palace. It is quite possible that during that visit he travelled to his sister's house in Kemsing.

The church of Kemsing was in need of restoration and it is believed that the first work was done on the chancel in the year 1260. Both Eleanor and Simon de Montfort were interested in the welfare of the parish and took some care in the appointment of a new Rector. This was a parson called Richard de Kemsing, which indicates that he was a locally born man. It is interesting to note that a later Rector of Ightham Church was called Robert de Kemsing, and one wonders if these two were, in fact, brothers.

Simon de Montfort was engaged in continuous warfare with his fellow barons against King Henry III and his son the Lord Edward, who later became King Edward I. This involved travelling from castle to castle throughout the country, and Countess Eleanor went with him to look after his household and the well-being of his followers. Among the castles they lived in was Odiham, Hampshire, where Eleanor, being a careful housekeeper, maintained a household roll, of which a section lasting from the nineteenth of February to the twenty-ninth of August 1265 is still extant. It includes a mention of fodder to be provided for four horses belonging to Richard de Kemsing, who is described there as a chaplain.

That year, Simon de Montfort fought his last battle at Evesham, Worcestershire, where he was killed and his body was mutilated. There is in Kemsing Church a gravestone which is of that period and by its design is described as a military tomb. For many years there was a local belief that this covered the body of Simon de Montfort. This is only a legend; Earl Simon's head was sent to Roger Mortimer's castle at Wigmore and his body was buried by the monks of Evesham, where his tomb became a place of pilgrimage. In any case the stone slab was moved to its present position in the sanctuary from somewhere in the nave during the restoration of 1870.

Countess Eleanor had to escape and she fled to Dover Castle, where for some period she was able to defend herself against the Royal party, assisted by her sons, Guy and Simon de Montfort. She later made a further escape to France, where she eventually died in Brittany in 1274, some nine years later.

Meanwhile, Richard de Kemsing, who is the first recorded Rector of Kemsing cum Seal, applied for and obtained the King's pardon, and his protection for a year. He remained Rector of Kemsing until his death in 1288.

One of Eleanor's ambitions was to build another church on her manor, but this she did not achieve, although one of her successors as Lord of the Manor was able to build Seal church in the year 1280, some six years after she had died. This venture was possibly inspired by her intentions.

One of the succeeding Lords of the Manor was Thomas de Grandison, who obtained a grant on the sixth of October 1366 from King Edward III for a weekly market on Mondays and an annual fair on the vigil, day and morrow of St. Peter and St. Paul the Apostle, near his manor next to Kemsing. This would appear to be a companion fair for Seal to the one already being held at Kemsing. Therefore, the people of the locality had weekly markets on two days, namely Monday at Seal and Wednesday at Kemsing. The fairs at Kemsing were probably held in the centre of the village. They ceased to be held during the puritan era of the Commonwealth, and were not regularly held after the restoration of King Charles II. In later centuries the venue was moved southwards to the area now covered by Fairfield Close.

In 1287, it is reported that there was a great storm throughout the south of England, in the course of which the whole town of Winchelsea in Sussex was submerged by the sea. While there is no record of how this affected the people of Kemsing, it is quite likely that many suffered from the loss of thatched roofs and of animals in the fields, as well as crops, hay-ricks and trees.

St Edith's Shrine

In the first half of the 13th century many changes were observed. Rood screens and lofts were introduced into English churches, and Kemsing was no exception. The lower half of the chancel screen represents part of that original rood screen, which would have been surmounted by a beam, on which the figures of Christ and St. Mary and St. John were imposed. Also, on the loft was a statue of St. Mary-the-Virgin. The rest of the church interior was highly decorated with wall paintings and three more statues, one to St.

Christopher and one each to St. Margaret and St. Catherine.

The positioning of these statues is not known, but their existence is proved by the wills of late fifteenth century farmers, who left money and goods to the church for the purpose of burning candles before each of these four statues.

The statue of St. Edith was outside the church in a small, separate shrine. By this time, the custom of making pilgrimages from Winchester and London to Canterbury to the shrine of St. Thomas a Becket, was becoming very popular. As Kemsing lay just to the south of the Pilgrims Way, which was one of many possible routes, some of these pilgrims would be obliged to come into the village for food and accommodation. It is possible that the people of Kemsing remembered then that they had a connection with St. Edith of Wilton, and by setting up her statue in a shrine, they attracted even more pilgrims, all of which was to the advantage of the village.

Again, the exact situation of this shrine is not known as it, together with all the statues, was destroyed in the late sixteenth century.

The porch was built on to the south wall of the church to cover the main entrance. This was at that time the site for marriages, which were performed at the door of the church in the open so that the public could be present.

One can only assume that a benefactor had this porch constructed for the advantage of members of the wedding parties to give them cover in the case of bad weather. The sides would be open without glazing, which enabled the public to observe and hear all that was going on. Such porches were being built throughout the country and were sometimes referred to as wedding porches.

The probable date given for this building is 1341 during the incumbency of Thomas de Hop, whose half brass can still be seen in the sanctuary. Also, during this period, a number of changes of ownership in the land throughout the parish was recorded by a married couple called Martin and Margery Peckham, who lived at Yaldham Manor. She was an Aldeham by birth, and she was inclined to acquire property wherever she could by means of accepting land in lieu of money when settling debts. She kept a roll, which records a great number of these transactions including many fields in the Kemsing Parish. *(See Appendix 15)*.

Throughout the thirteen hundreds, there must have been a fair amount of traffic along the Pilgrims Way, because the Archbishops of Canterbury had houses situated at intervals along the main roads of the country so that they could break their journeys from one Cathedral City to another, and from Canterbury to London there were two of these Manor Houses which affected Kemsing, one at Wrotham and one at Otford.

There is therefore no doubt that processions of some magnitude would have progressed along the Pilgrims Way, and according to the weather maybe even through the village. One evidence of this is revealed by the finding in 1950 of the metal seal of a papal bull or edict of Pope Clement VI, dated 1342, in a field on the Pilgrims Way.

The year 1348 saw the outbreak of the Black Death in Europe, following several years of poor harvests, epidemics of animal diseases, and climatic deterioration. No-one knows to what extent all this affected Kemsing. Thomas de Hop the Rector died in 1347. At the time of his last illness, he was involved in a dispute about tithes with Richard Wastan of Seal, but he died before the case was settled.

The new Rector was William de Penebrugge, but of his activity during the Black Death nothing is known. One effect of this devastating plague was the cessation of highly decorative work in churches, which perhaps contributed to the introduction of what is known as the perpendicular style, which is simpler. Kemsing's windows are mostly perpendicular and so they date from the 14th or 15th Centuries. The few examples of old glass still to be seen in the church are of the fourteenth and fifteenth centuries.

Another effect of the plague was the change in agricultural pursuits. Because labour became short, intensive farming such as corn growing was to some extent abandoned in favour of the running of sheep. Kemsing then had a "corn and sheep" economy, with sheep being folded on the stubble after harvest, to provide manure, to which the midden manure from stalled animals was an addition. This change of agricultural policy was eventually advantageous, and farmers in the district in the following century were undoubtedly much better off than their predecessors.

The tenancy of the Rectorship changed frequently at this period, according to the wishes of the holders. There is an example, in which the Rector was able to lease the church for two years to two other priests, one called John Diggs, the other Robert de la Beche, at a rate of £30 per annum. Robert de la Beche at that time was also Rector of Ightham, and between them these two had to provide a chaplain for Kemsing and Seal. This arrangement was not approved of by the patron of the living, who was Sir Thomas Grandison, Lord of the Manor, and he presented a third man, Thomas Perd, to take their place. This created a situation in which three of four Clerks in Holy Orders all purported to be Rector of Kemsing at the same time. The end of the fourteenth century saw the changeover between the word Rector and Vicar for the incumbent of Kemsing church. The income of a Rector was derived from the payment of tithes by certain of his parishioners. Tithes were normally one tenth of a landowner's or a tenant's proceeds for a year, and they were usually paid in kind. The right to present a priest to a "living" was held by the owner of an "Advowson", who could be the Lord of the Manor, or a wealthy magnate, or even the Crown. This had become an asset, liable for sale as a whole or in part, thus becoming a valuable property. In 1397, it was held by one Guido de Mone, who sold it to the Priory and Convent of St. Saviour in Bermondsey. Soon after this the Priory became an Abbey, the Prior became an Abbot, and he received the tithes and appointed a priest to the living of Kemsing, to act vicariously for the Abbey as Vicar for an agreed stipend.

The Rector-designate was a man called Adam of Usk, who contested the right of the Abbey to his title. His story is of great interest.

Chapter 3
Under Lancastrian And Yorkist Kings

Adam Of Usk

Adam was born at Usk in Monmouthshire about AD 1352. He found a patron in Edmund Mortimer, Earl of March, who was connected with the Royal family, and who helped Adam to go to Oxford to read law. Here he eventually secured a doctorate and stayed on as a don. In 1388, however, he was involved in a student riot when he sided with the Welsh students and the southerners against the northerners. After a few days of fighting, many of the students were sent down. After being ordained into Holy Orders, Adam held several livings, but was never a parish priest. These livings he was apt to exchange when it suited him, so he became in turn Rector of Mitchel Troy in Monmouthshire; Babcary in Somerset, Castle Combe in Wiltshire, and Hanningfield in Essex.

These were followed by livings at Shire Newton, Monmouthshire, and Panteg, Monmouthshire, which he obtained from one of his cousins, and passed on to yet another cousin. He kept a chronicle, in which is an entry "in these days my Lord of Canterbury *(Archbishop Arundel)* bestowed upon me the goodly church of Kemsing, along with the chapel of Seal in Kent, and another goodly prebend".

He also gave to one of his cousins, Sir Thomas Adam Ap William of Weloe, the church of Shire Newton in Gwent, and to another cousin Sir Matthew Ap Heol the church of Panteg. He did not enjoy Kemsing for long because he had enemies, particularly among the members of the Arundel family. He struggled to hold Kemsing, which was valued at some thirty marks, but was not successful, because the Abbot of Bermondsey, having acquired the advowson, was prepared to institute a vicar.

A Papal mandate to the Archbishop of Canterbury stated that the church and the chapel at Seal had been appropriated to the Abbey of St. Saviour, Bermondsey, but on a representation by Adam that divine service in these churches had been neglected, the Pope annulled the appropriation. Thereupon the Abbey petitioned again upon the grounds of wrongful dispossession on false pretences. This time judgement was given in favour of the Abbey, and an order was given for the removal of Adam of Usk. To ensure that fresh litigation should not be entered into, the abbot persuaded the Pope to make the appropriation order anew. Thus Adam's term of office at Kemsing came to an end, but his subsequent activities are so interesting that they are worth recording here.

He had become very officious and not always as wise as he was learned. He believed in prophecies and signs and portents, and he dreamed curious dreams. He became a state official and a Member of Parliament, and was present at the coronation of King Henry IV, after having served on the commission that advised the deposition of King Richard II.

Then a curious thing happened. For a reason not easy to explain, he descended to common theft. In 1402, he and two others stole a horse and a bag containing a hundred shillings in Westminster. King Henry IV had never been very fond of Adam and this behaviour caused him to have Adam convicted as a common thief and exiled. Adam chose Rome as his destination, where after many hard experiences in crossing the continent and in particular the Alps, he made himself useful as a lawyer and soon made himself money.

He hoped to influence the suit which he was prosecuting at the Papal Court for the recovery of the Rectory of Kemsing and Seal. When the case went against him, he persuaded the Pope to make him Archdeacon of Buckingham, and Vicar of Knoyle, Tisbury and Deverill; also, Archdeacon of Llandaff, Vicar of Llandefailog, and Prebendary of Llanbiston. He was still unpopular in England, and none of these titles benefited him. He had to confess that he was not advanced but abased by these titles, became very poor, and was stripped of any benefit. His character is revealed by the final sentence in his chronicle about this time, namely, "however, I was paid with gold for my counsel". During his six years in exile, he witnessed the election of Pope Innocent VII, from whom he tried to gain the Bishopric of St. Davids, but failed. His last activity in Rome was to secure help for the convent of Usk, where several of his relatives and friends were nuns.

Then the Pope fell into trouble, and without his patronage Adam was obliged to leave Rome, which he did disguised as a sailor in order to thwart his persecutors. He made his way north, but had to wait in Amiens for two years, while he tried to persuade Henry IV to let him return to England. The permission failed to arrive, so he landed illegally in Wales and hid up in the hills until his pardon came in 1411. He went straight back to London and took his seat in Parliament.

Archbishop Arundel gave him the living of Merstham in Surrey in place of all the other livings which he had lost during his exile. He witnessed a second coronation, that of Henry V. When his friend the Archbishop died in 1414, Adam wrote "who gave me the good churches of Kempsing in Kent and Merstham in Surrey, together with the prebend of Llandogo in Wales, and through whom I was hoping for promotion to greater things".

He made several changes of living after this, and finally died only two miles away from his native Usk, where he was buried. Consistent with his lifelong ability to make himself a nuisance, his brass in that church has proved baffling to everyone who has tried to read it. It is just a strip of metal, with two lines engraved on it in Welsh, but so written and so full of spelling mistakes, that it has never been properly translated. He would no doubt have been soothed and flattered could he have foreseen that his epitaph, probably composed by himself, would cause so much learned discussion in after ages.

The First Vicar

During the first half of the fifteenth century many changes were made in the village of Kemsing. The west door and the west window of the church were inserted by cutting out a section of the wall and refilling round them with thinner material. The actual structure of the west wall was quite different from the structure of the south wall, which indicates that it in its turn had not been there for very many years.

The south doorway which was originally a tall Saxon style arch, may also have been altered at this time, although that change may not have been made until the seventeenth century when the wall above the door cracked and had to be repaired. The appropriation of the church at Kemsing and the chapel at Seal to the Abbey at Bermondsey was ratified to the Archbishop of Canterbury by a papal bull, or edict, whereupon the Abbot instituted Rodelandus Kerbroke as the first Vicar of Kemsing and Seal. He was replaced over the years by John Jordan in 1417, Thomas Stowe in 1422, Richard Litelman in 1437, John Gossick in 1438, and Henry Esthaw in 1445.

Some indication of the life of tradesmen in country villages at this time is given by an order made by the sheriff of Southampton in 1418, for the arrest of Roger of Kemsing, sometimes known as Robert Kemsyng, and some others who were carpenters. They had been told to serve the King, Henry VI, in their "artefices and misteries" but they had bolted back to Kemsing after receiving their final wages. Such tradesmen were obliged to travel away from their homes if required to do so by their overlords.

The Lordship of the Manor of Kemsing had by now passed to the Fiennes family who became Lords Say and Sele. On the fourth of July 1450, James Fiennes, who owned Knole and Hever, was killed by the followers of Jack Cade, who had led a revolt against King Henry VI, which culminated in the battle of Solefields, near Sevenoaks. How far Kemsing people were involved in this insurrection is not recorded, but both villages benefited in that Fiennes left in his will "twenty marks for the works of the church at Kemsinge and Sele".

PROSPEROUS FARMERS

During this part of the century, many houses were being built in Kemsing, possibly including the east end of West House, part of Ivy Farmhouse, the west end of Malt House, letterbox end of Nearly Corner, Walnut Tree Cottage, Broughton, and a Tudor rebuild of St. Clere, which was later demolished to be replaced by the present building.

The ravages of the disastrous pestilence or bubonic plague which had raged through Europe and this country in 1348 and 1349, known since Victorian times as the Black Death, were gradually being overcome. The ending of the long drawn out wars against France also helped to bring in a more settled period when labour was more plentiful. The evidence of many wills made at this time indicates that farming was becoming a prosperous industry. As has been seen, these wills also give information about the church and the shrine of St. Edith, which had been built maybe in the end of the 14th century, because they include bequests of money and goods for the benefit of the church and of the shrine. For instance, William Fremlin asked in his will to be buried "in the churchyard of St. Mary-the-Virgin at Kemsing", which proves that the dedication of the church was to St. Mary and not to St. Edith as was commonly believed for several centuries up to the late nineteenth century.

Extracts from some of these wills make interesting reading, viz:-

FROM THE WILL OF JOHN FREMELYN OF KEMSYNG CO. KENT DATED THE SIXTH OF MAY 1457:-

"Likewise I bequeath to the high altar of the same church for tithes and oblations many times negligently forgotton 8d.
Likewise I bequeath to the light of St. Katherine of the same church 1 sheep
Likewise I bequeath to the light of St. Margaret there 1 sheep
Likewise I bequeath for the use and convenience of the chapel of St. Ede of Kemsyng 1 sheep".

From the will of William Smyth of Eversham parish of Kemsyng co. Kent dated the fourth of April 1458:-
"Likewise I bequeath to the high altar of the same church for forgotten tithes 40d.
Likewise I bequeath for the repair of the chapel of Edith being in the churchyard of Kemsyng 40d.
Likewise I bequeath 1 cow for the maintenance of one trundel-wheel in the parish church of Kemsyng for ever".

From the will of Walter Fremlyng of Kemsyng dated the twentieth of December 1459:-
"I bequeath ... seven candles to burn in the church & the chapel of St. Edyth that is to say one to burn before the cross & 1 before the likeness of St. Edith & 2 before the likeness of St. Katherine & 2 before the likeness of St. Margaret & 1 before the likeness of St. Christopher in the said church of Kemsyng".

From the will of John Meller of Eversham in the parish of Kemsyng dated the twelfth of May 1459:-
"And that they pay to Richard Chown 4d. & that they pay to John Cogger 3s. & that they pay towards the repair of the trundle-wheel of Kemsyng aforesaid 16d. And that they pay towards the light of the Blessed Virgin Mary at Kemsyng aforesaid 7d. And that they pay towards the repair of the chapel of St. Edith being in the churchyard of Kemsyng 10d".

From the will of John Ivott of Kemsyng diocese of Rochester dated Monday after the Feast of the Purification of the Blessed

Virgin Mary 1463:-
"Likewise I bequeath to the high altar there for my tithes forgotton or wrongly retained 20d. Likewise I bequeath to the light in front of the high cross in the same church 1 candle of one pound. Likewise I bequeath to the light of St. Margaret in the same church 1 candle of one pound. Likewise I bequeath for the repair of the books of the parish church of Kemsyng aforesaid 12d. Likewise I bequeath for two torches to be provided for the church of Kemsyng aforesaid within a year after my decease 13s.4d.
And concerning the money arising therefrom I will that five marks be disposed for a suitable chaplain to celebrate for my soul in the church of Kemsyng aforesaid for half a year".

From the will of John Smyth of Everham in the parish of Kemsing dated the twentieth of June 1471:-
"First I leave my soul to Almighty God the Blessed Virgin Mary &c. Likewise I leave to the high altar there for my forgotten tithes 12d. Likewise I leave to the cathedral church of Rochester 6d. Likewise I leave to the chapel of St. Edith one lamb".

In 1463, the Fiennes family disposed of the Lordship of the Manor to Sir Geoffrey Bullen, the grandfather of Queen Anne Boleyn. It is generally thought that this purchase also included the house and estate at Crowdleham. The Bullens were Lords of the Manor until the execution of George Boleyn, the brother of Queen Anne in 1556, when the Lordship reverted to the Crown, in the person of King Henry VIII.

In 1487, the St. Clere estate and house were appropriated by King Henry VII *(the former owners, descendants of Sir John de St. Clere having died out during the Wars of the Roses)* and given to one of his "new men" called Henry Lovell. The latter demolished the old building and rebuilt it in brick in the new style. This building was to remain for a further hundred years until it was rebuilt again in the early 17th century.

KEMSING
KENT
CANTERBURY
PILGRIMS WAY

Chapter 4
The Tudor Period

A Colourful Church

The sixteenth century started well for Kemsing. The apparent wealth of the farmers, as indicated by the terms of their wills in the latter part of the previous century, meant that more and more houses were being built or extended. Among these can be included "Castle Bank", "The Keep", "Rose" and "Well Cottages". "Wybournes Cottages", "Dormer Cottage", Nos 47 and 49 West End, the Vicarage, the middle range of "The Malthouse", the north wing of "Walnut Tree Cottage", part of "Nearly Corner", the first floor of "Broughton", and parts of "Crowdleham". Also at St. Clere was the newly built brick house, erected by Henry Lovell in place of the old house of the de Aldeham and St. Clere families. All these developments meant increased work for the people of the village and of Heverham.

The church was at its most beautiful with coloured glass in the windows, wall paintings and coloured statues of St. Margaret, St. Mary, St. Catherine and St. Christopher. In the churchyard, the shrine of St. Edith with its statue of the saint and, reputedly a relic in the form of one of her arms, was attracting pilgrims from afar, as well as the local people who resorted to it for help with problems of their health and that of their crops.

Difficult Times For The Clergy

During this century, no less than twelve vicars served the parish, eleven of them for an average of only about five years each because the last, Gilbert Gennyns, was vicar for the final thirty-nine years of the century. This meant that there was continual change and that, combined with the changing patterns of the organisation of the Church of England at the Reformation, must have caused the people of Kemsing a great deal of confusion and distress.

These twelve vicars who held the incumbency throughout the Tudor period had much to contend with. William Lincoln was instituted on the 27th August 1508 in the place of William Yanson, who had died in office, and was probably buried in Seal church or churchyard *(as were William Lincoln and Thomas Taylour)*. This is another indication of the ascendancy of Seal village and church over those of Kemsing, a fact that endured right up to the nineteenth century. It was not until the twentieth century that the population of Kemsing outgrew that of Seal.

William Lincoln had served as vicar for only a year before he died, and his successor Nicholas Metcalfe was instituted on 31st October 1509, the patron being the Abbot of Bermondsey. He resigned the living in 1517, and his successor Richard Sharpe was instituted on 27th October that year. He, in turn, resigned in 1524 to be succeeded by Thomas Theobald, whose long term as vicar was marked by frequent absences, not only from the parish but from the country, as he travelled on intelligence work for the King. He was a local man, related to the Theobald family who lived for many years in Dynes Farm and at Stonepitts.

Theobald was followed by John Denman, who seems to have been instituted twice, in 1545 and again in 1548. The circumstances of this are not known but are indicative of the troubled times through which the church was going. Denman exchanged the living for another one with Thomas Hicklyng. The latter was vicar from 28th November 1550 to 24th April 1554, when he was deprived of the living by the newly enthroned Queen

Mary Tudor, who replaced him with her nominee, Thomas Taylour. Taylour died four years later and was succeeded by another nominee of the Queen who had assumed the role of patron of the living after the dissolution of the Abbey of Bermondsey, awarding the Rectorial Tithes to her cousin, Cardinal Pole. The new man was Thomas Dale, and he served as vicar from 1558 to 31st October 1561, when Gilbert Gennyns or Jenyns, was appointed by the new Queen, Elizabeth the First.

The divorce of Henry VIII from Catherine of Aragon in 1533 brought about his decision to part from allegiance to the Pope and to make himself and his successors Head of the Church in England. This made little difference to ordinary people for some years. The services continued in Latin as before, but by 1537, Thomas Cranmer was drafting a new prayer book in English. King Henry had already, in 1536, ordered that all parishes should provide a bible that was available for everyone in the parish to read. Another order went out in 1538 to the effect that all parishes must keep registers of baptisms, marriages and burials, but many seem to have ignored this.

The Vicar of Kemsing at that time was that Thomas Theobald whose extensive travels on the continent meant that he had no time to take steps to implement the new law in Kemsing and Seal.

The order was repeated in 1547 and again in 1559, but it was not until 1561 that the first register was opened in Kemsing. The years between had all been troublesome ones, and the five vicars who served between Thomas Theobald and Gilbert Gennyns had had much change to contend with. The accession of Edward VI in 1547 saw a rapid change from the Roman Catholicism of the past to the new Anglo Catholicism, and in 1549 the Vicar, John Denman, had to accept the new prayer book in English and also the disappearance of St. Edith's Day, the 16th September, from the Church Calendar. This latter must have caused considerable feeling in the parish, where the shrine to St. Edith still stood in the churchyard.

Two years after this, in the first year of office of Thomas

Hicklyng, King Edward VI ordered all church plate to be surrendered to the State. Whether Kemsing church was thus deprived, is not known, but there is no church plate now extant in Kemsing older than 1564, when a silver chalice made by John Clarke of the Goldsmiths Company in London was presented to the church.

Had Kemsing obeyed a further instruction in 1562 to make an inventory of all its goods, the existence of any silver hallmarked before 1551 would be known, but there is no record of such an inventory for this parish.

By this time, the religious practice of the country had become more stabilised, and Gennyns probably maintained an even level of churchmanship for the people of Kemsing right up to his resignation in January 1602, forty-two years after his institution. This does not mean that he was often present in either village of Kemsing or Seal for, on 5th December 1570, he became Rector of Sevenoaks, and he was also the vicar of St. Dunstan in the West in the City of London, and Rector of Little Parndon in Essex. To hold these offices, he must have employed a number of curates and assistant priests, but which of these looked after Kemsing is not known.

When he was instituted in 1561, Gennyns seems to have taken steps to comply with the order about keeping registers, for the first of these for baptisms began with the entry, "1561 October 4th, Joan daughter of John Akourt". The first entry in the register of burials read, "1562, May 26th, Elizabeth daughter of Thomas Fyllder", and that for marriages read, "1562, November 2nd, John Ffremllyn the Elder, maryed to Margret Scrakes".

Meanwhile, the Lordship of the Manor had been changing hands, largely as the result of national events. From Geoffrey Bullen, who had acquired it in 1463, it had descended to Ann Boleyn's father, Thomas Bullen, Earl of Wiltshire, and then to his son, George Bullen, Lord Rochford, who was executed for his complicity in the events that led up to the execution of his sister Anne. Thereafter, the Lordship reverted to the Crown, and in 1541, Henry VIII nominated it as one of the manors set aside to provide revenues for the upkeep of the household of Queen Anne of Cleves after her divorce from the King. When she died in 1558, Elizabeth I was on the throne, and she granted the Lordship to her cousin, Henry Carey, Lord Hunsdon.

Various orders in council were made during the Tudor period governing the civil conduct of the land. In 1536, parishes were ordered to undertake responsibility for the welfare of their impotent poor. Branding vagrants had been usual practice for many years, and was still allowed in 1547; and in 1572 the overseers of the parish branded vagrants on the shoulder. Parish constables were empowered to arrest such vagrants in 1597, when Justices of the Peace appointed overseers of the poor through the vestry meeting.

The maintenance of public roads was made the responsibility of the local authority by an Act of Parliament made in 1554. Surveyors were appointed and ten years later, and again in 1586, the Act was extended and the responsibilities increased. The 1564 Act stated that roads must be maintained by local authority, either by "statute", i.e. residents giving six days unpaid work a year, or by levying a rate for the labour. The 1586 Act was mostly concerned with the making of new roads.

Outside the parish, apart from the manifold changes in the politics of the country, other things were happening which must have influenced the lives of people in small villages like Kemsing. Two maps of Kent were issued. One by Saxton in 1579, and one by Symonson of Rochester in 1596. The latter shows Kemsing Park but no church at Woodlands. This was because the church there had declined into ruin, since the ravages of the Black Death in 1348, and it was no longer a viable parish. On the continent, the Julian Calendar was abandoned for the Gregorian Calendar, which left England's dates ten days behind. This deficit was eventually remedied in 1752 when eleven days were "lost" in order to catch up with the continental calendar.

In 1593, the statute mile of 1760 yards was established.

BULLEN

LEADING FAMILIES

From some of the wills made at this time, it is possible to learn about the residences of some of the leading families of Kemsing. For instance John Theobald mentioned in 1546 that John Miller was occupying Dynes Farm which was owned by the Theobald family, and also that Gilbert Miller occupied Cotmans Ash. A later will *(1551)* of Gilbert Miller reveals that he owned a tenement known as "Castle Bank" which was probably let to tenants because he stipulated that his widow, Joan, should have the rents therefrom until his son Richard reached the age of twenty-one. Another family mentioned was called Wybourne, which may give rise to the naming of the old house called "Wybournes".

Looking through the entries in the three parish registers, of Baptisms, Marriages, and Burials, it is possible to pick out the largest families, from their numerous references in all three books. By combining such entries with the knowledge already gained of ownership and occupation, it is possible to assess which families were most prominent in terms of wealth and influence. Of these there are the Theobalds owning Stonepitts and Dynes; the Millers owning Castle Bank and Cotmans Ash and other houses; the Fremlyns occupying West House and several other houses. Among others were the Kipps family, marking the beginnings of their five-hundred year residence in the village. Wigzells, Bakers, Hartrops, Carters, Taylors, and Allens, all flourished here for many years to come.

As already mentioned the village was on the direct route from Wrotham to Otford, in both of which were Archbishops Palaces so there would have been occasions when large bodies of people attending important men progressed, either along the top Pilgrims Road, or through the village on the direct route between the churches of Kemsing and Otford. One such procession accompanied Cardinal Campeggio in July 1518, when he was on his way from Dover to London to attend a conference on European affairs. It is likely that some of the retinue of Henry VIII lodged in or went through Kemsing in late 1532 when the King was on the way to meet Francis I of France at the field of the Cloth of Gold.

At Stonepitts lived Reynolds Carter who in his will asked for a torch to be burnt in honour of St. Edith in the chapel in Kemsing churchyard, and he also mentioned other Kemsing residents, including his son, Reynolds Junior, William Fremlyn Junior, Thomas Reeve, Robert and Gilbert Miller, Robert Robyns, Thomas Barns, and William Watts. Perhaps the John Fuller whom he also mentions as living at Seal gave his name to the present Fullers Street above Tanners Cross.

At St. Clere, other changes of ownership were made throughout the century. Henry Lovell, the builder of the Tudor-style brick house, had died leaving the estate to two daughters, Agnes and Elizabeth. Agnes was the wife of John Empson, a cousin of Henry VIII's financial adviser, Richard Empson. She sold her half of the property to Sir Thomas Bullen, Queen Anne Boleyn's father who lived at Hever. Elizabeth was married to Anthony Windsor, who sold her half of the property to Richard Farmer. The latter negotiated with Sir Thomas Bullen for his half, and eventually united the two again, but sold the whole to George Moulton of Hadlow, who had married Agnes Polhill of Sevenoaks, and whose sister Jane was married to William Lambarde of Sevenoaks. The Moultons remained in possession of St. Clere until 1625. The St. Clere estate formed a community sufficient to itself, and any allegiance it had to a village would have been to Ightham as it was at that time in Ightham parish. So the people of Kemsing were not likely to have been affected by the changes at St. Clere, although those who lived at Heverham might well have depended on the large house for employment.

The last years of the Tudor period were not so good in Kemsing as the opening years of the 16th century had been. Because of the many changes in religious practice, and the many ups and downs in the government of the country as a whole, life was not too easy for villagers, some of whom may have been involved as serving soldiers or sailors in the many wars. In 1558, beacons burned throughout the countryside to warn of the coming of the Spanish Armada, and it is more than likely that one of these was built on the hill above the village.

The shrine to St. Edith in the churchyard must have been destroyed before 1570 because William Lambarde, when visiting Kemsing during his peregrination of Kent in that year, wrote in his "A Perambulation of Kent" , "in the late time of the Popish *(religion)*, the image of Edith *(the daughter of King Edgar)* was religiously frequented in the churchyard at Kemsing, for the preservation of corne and graine, from blasting, myldew, brandeare, and such other harmes as commonly do annoy it". By using the word Popish, he probably referred to the reign of Queen Mary Tudor from 1554 to 1558, although in a remote village like Kemsing, those practices might well have been in use well into the reign of Queen Elizabeth I. Unfortunately, Lambarde gave very little information about the village, apart from the negative news that in his lists of "forrestes and parks, hilles and fayres, and castles" Kemsing is not mentioned. He noted that the parish was in the Lathe of Sutton-at-Home in the Hundred of Coddeshethe which latter comprised "the towns of Shorham, Halsted, Otteford, Woodland, Sundrishe, Sevenoke, Kemsynge, Seale, Cheveninge, Leighe and Spelherst". He also found that Kemsing was the mother church and "Seale but a childe, *(chappell)* of it".

The rest of his report was taken up by a diatribe about the foolishness of the people of this village, comparing them with some old Romans who were said to have held in great veneration a certain god called Robigus to whom they offered intercessions and sacrifices for the preservation and delivery of their grain from the selfsame annoyance as those here. He was also sceptical of the role played by the priest of the parish at that time, who having received a peck or two of corn from "some seelie bodie" offered it to the image of the saint and then took the greater portion for himself "*(for you must consider he would bee sure to gaine by the bargaine)*". He would then give back the smaller portion to be mingled with the seedcorn rendering the whole sowing safe from harm.

KEMSING
KENT
CANTERBURY
PILGRIMS WAY

Chapter 5
The 17th Century Or The Stuart Period

Civil War And The Plague

In this century many more houses were built and old ones extended. These included Foster House, Yew Tree House, the barn at The Chequers, St. Clere, parts of Ivy Farm House, Malthouse, Broughton, Lower St. Clere, West House and the Box House.

The Revd. Richard Buckley, who was Vicar from 1602 to 1608 was followed by the Revd. Robert Baker, in whose time, according to the Revd. F.S. Frampton who researched and wrote in 1892, "the old 5th bell in Seal church was cast in 1609 by Stephen Swan". He does not mention a bell or bells in Kemsing church, but Kemsing's oldest bell was cast at about this time.

Robert Baker's successor as vicar, was the Revd. John Baker who may have been his son or other relative. This Mr. Baker cared for the parish for the period up to the beginning of the Civil War in 1642. These were years of change in both national and local affairs. The throne was now occupied by King Charles I, whose quarrels with Parliament resulted in the outbreak of Civil War. Within the Church of England many changes were brought about by the policies of Archbishop Laud of Canterbury.

There was considerable sickness from time to time which culminated in the Great Plague of London in 1665. In Seal, some sixteen people had died of bubonic plague in 1611, but there is no record of any such deaths in Kemsing. Eight burials were registered in the years 1665 and 1666, but there is no indication of the cause of death. Only one of these is marked by a stone, the oldest legible one in the churchyard. It commemorates Joan Chapman, a widow. Earlier, in 1636, there had been an outbreak of plague in Riverhead. According to Derek Turner's book "The Black Death" *(Longman's "Then and There" Series)*, "in Kent the Gayle family was beginning to make its fortune by working hard, saving money, and gradually building up a flourishing blacksmiths' business for goods made of iron which were much in demand at the time. Francis Gayle, head of the family, had plenty of sons to carry on and expand the business. One of his sons, Leonard, wrote in his old age the following story:

I was born in the parish of Sevenoaks in Kent, my father a blacksmith living in Riverhead Street, in the parish aforesaid, drove a very good trade. My mother was the daughter of George Pratt a very good yeoman living at Chelsfield about five miles from Riverhead. My father had by a former wife two sons, and by my mother three sons and one daughter, and when I was between sixteen and seventeen years of age my father and mother going to visit a friend at Kemsing in the said county, took the plague and quickly after they came home my mother fell sick and about six days later she died, nobody thinking of such a disease. My father made a great burial for her, and many people came to it not fearing anything, and no manner of clothes were taken out of the chamber when she died, but not one of them present took the distemper. This I put down as a miracle. After her burial, we were all well one week, and a great many people frequented our house and we our neighbours' houses. But at the week's end, in two days my father, my eldest brother, my sister and myself fell sick and in three days after this, my two younger brothers fell sick. Though I was very ill my father sent me to market to buy provisions, but before I came home it was noised abroad that it was the plague, and as soon as I came indoors they charged us to keep in and they set a strong watch over us. Yet all this while no-one else took the distemper from us. About the sixth day, after they were taken, three of them died within three hours, one after another and were buried in one grave. All this while I lay sick in another bed, and the nurse looked every hour for my death, but it pleased God most miraculously to preserve me and without any sore breaking. Only I had a swelling in my groin which it was long ere it sunk away, and I have been the worse for it ever since. When I recovered, I was shut up with two women, one man and one child for three months, and neither of them had the distemper".

This story had a happy ending, for after a difficult two years when Leonard was down to the last £50 of the £200 he had inherited, things began to improve. When he died at the age of sixty-nine, he left to his five children, £16,000, a shop, and a blacksmith's forge near Crawley in Sussex.

Several records of land and property holdings mentioned the names of families living in the parish and the location of their homes. At Clavvokisden lived John and Joan Monk with one son Jack. The house became known as "Monks-in-the-hole" *(since renamed "Oaklea" in Birchin Cross Road)*. In Stub Crouch *(now renamed Chart Rise)* at the top of the rise in West End from Childsbridge Lane, lived a member of the large family of Kipps, Richard, who was in dispute with David Polhill of Otford over one or two parcels of land. The old parsonage house on the site of the present Vicarage Cottages was described in a terrier of 1634 as holding eight rooms with a garden and orchard, covering sixteen rods, or about four acres of glebe land. The location of the old Kemsing Park was shown on three of the many maps of Kent made in the seventeenth century. The first in1608 showed both Kemsing and Otford churches standing outside the boundaries of the Park, as does another dated 1614. In 1634 John Harrison also marked the Park on a map of the Lathe of Sutton at Hone and the Hundred of Codsheath. At St. Clere, the old Tudor building was rebuilt in the new style similar to the new house at Chevening, and the property was sold by the Moulton family to Sir John Sidley. It is recorded that the final stage in the rebuilding was the dedication of the chapel by Bishop Bancroft in 1633, but the situation of this reputed chapel has not been established.

Bunce Memorials pre 1890

SACKVILLES AND BUNCES

It was at this time that the Lordship of the Manor passed into the Sackville family. It had been held by the Careys since Lord Hunsdon's time, being handed down through Henry Carey to his son George, who in turn left it to his brother John. The latter left it to his son, another Henry Carey, who eventually sold it to Richard Sackville. For a while it was leased to one Henry Smith, but a later Sackville recovered the title and it remained in the Sackville-West family until recent years. The outbreak of Civil War in 1642 might well have caused much heartsearching in Kemsing, among those who may have been of an age to be involved in the fighting. Living at St. Clere was the very staunch Parliamentarian, Sir John Sidley, who was a member of the County Commission of Sequestration, set up to collect fines and sequester estates from Royalist rebels who took part in an uprising in Kent in 1643. He collected fines from a number of Shoreham residents to the tune of £29. From the lists of those involved, there is no evidence of Kemsing men being apprehended even if they took part.

Crowdleham at that time was owned by James Bunce although he did not reside there. According to Hasted's "History of Kent" he was Sheriff of London in 1643 and a Member of the Fishmongers Company. In fact he was Master of the Leathersellers Company, where he is still well remembered. Gifts of money and goods are even now distributed from charities which he founded. When he died in 1670 his funeral cortege left from the Leathersellers Hall on its way to St. Benet's Church in Gracechurch Street. Being a steady Royalist and refusing to comply with the establishment of a Commonwealth in England, he with the Lord Mayor and others was committed to the Tower on 25th September 1647. He lost all his offices and his estates were forfeited. Obliged to leave the country, he joined the Royalist circle in the Low Countries where in 1650 King Charles II granted him the rank of Baronet for his services to the Royalist cause. He is said to have neglected to register this warrant for the title of baronet, but styled himself Sir James, and his son and grandsons likewise called themselves Sir John, Sir John and Sir James. The last named paid a tribute to his grandfather when he raised a monument to the family in the chancel of St. Mary's church *(now in the choir vestry)*. That part which extols the virtues of the first Sir James reads:-

> "In this chancel and family vault are deposited the remains of Sir James Bunce, Bart., lineally descended from James Bunce, Alderman of London who in the troubled times of King Charles II assisted that unhappy monarch with 60,000 pounds an immense sum in those days and also at his own expense raised maintained clothed and paid a troop of horse for his defence. But the Alderman with many more of the King's friends were obliged to quit this country and to retire into foreign parts with the King who being at Faulkeland in Bred in July 1650 his Majesty there conferred on him the honour and title of Baronet of this Realm. The Alderman's estates being very considerable in the counties of Kent, Essex, Surrey, Middlesex and in the City of London, were sequestrated by that Arch Traitor Oliver Cromwell. But on the happy restoration he was put into possession of those in Kemsing, Seal, Chimbhams,

and Otterden in this county and others in the City of London with about £7,000 in part of the monies that he had advanced to the King who in consideration of his services granted him and his heirs a pension of £400 per annum which was regularly paid until Sir Robert Walpole's administration". (1727).

After the execution of King Charles I in 1649, the full effect of Parliamentary rule was felt in Kemsing and Seal. Any last trace of ornamentation in the churches was removed, and a period of solemn dress and behaviour was introduced. The Vicar, the Revd. John Baker, was evicted in 1650 and two of Cromwell's "parsons" were appointed. One called Master Marten was to look after Seal, which then became quite a separate parish from Kemsing, where Master Bartton was put in charge. A Commission was formed with the duty of drawing up details of the various parsonage properties held in Kemsing and Seal. One of these, standing where Vicarage Cottages are now in St. Edith's Road, was described as being "impropriate" *(i.e. not used as a vicarage)* and in the possession of James Bunce of Crowdleham, who let it to William Kipps. This latter was probably William, born 1614, the son of Richard and father of John, Matthew and Richard, who died in 1693.

One who suffered much from the changes in religious and political observance in the seventeenth century was the Revd. Dr. Michael Jermin, whose memorial is on the south wall of the chancel in St. Mary's Church. He was a native of Exeter, where his grandfather had been Mayor and where his father Alexander was a merchant and a sheriff of the city. Educated at Oxford, Michael took a Doctorate at Leyden University and was a writer of many books. As Chaplain to the Princess Elizabeth, daughter of James I and later Electress of Hanover, and thus the direct ancestor of our present Queen, he was close to the Royal family, and he was eventually appointed Chaplain to King Charles I. As a staunch royalist he was out of favour with the Parliamentarian authorities and was ejected from his livings of St. Martin's, Ludgate Hill and of Edgburton in Sussex. Much of his property was sequestrated and he had to come to Kemsing to live with his daughter Rachel and her husband John Theobald, at Dynes. One day in 1659 he went to Sevenoaks to preach there and on his return journey he fell from his horse and died. His daughter Rachel had six children of whom only one survived. The inscription on his memorial is in Latin and can be roughly translated as:

> "Hail, observer, who bends his light to peer.
> "Whose place is this?" you ask; he, whose place this is, himself reveals. Servant I am; yet Christ has added Master (i.e. D.D.) in addition to that; even if the grander title does not befit me, let not the lesser be unfitting.
> MICHAEL JERMIN is the name with which he was born; dust and bones no longer attract those titles. Farewell".

Master Bartton's activities in the parish seem to have come to an end in 1654, when a new vicar was appointed. He was the Revd. John Stevens, and his first duty was to take on the registration of baptisms, marriages and burials, a duty which was sometimes neglected during the Commonwealth. An order had been issued in 1652 to the effect that registrars for this purpose were to be elected by parishioners, and in the case of Seal the new incumbent was chosen for the office, which was the exception rather than the rule. The people of Kemsing seem to have elected a layman as Registrar, for the records of three marriages in 1656 include the words "before me, Nicholas Fremlin, Clark and Regester". Kemsing's registers had been in being since 1561, but the registers for Seal began in 1654.

John Stevens was Vicar for fourteen years, which meant that he saw the restoration of King Charles II in 1660. This event may have dismayed some Kemsing families, but doubtless brought comfort to others, who had resented the strict rule of the Commonwealth, which forbade the wearing of coloured clothing, the enjoyment of maypole dancing and similar activities, and the holding of the old fairs such as the St. Edith Fair in September. In 1668 Mr. Stevens resigned the living and was succeeded by the Revd. Thomas Stevens. It was not unusual for sons to follow fathers, but there is no evidence that this was the case here. Unfortunately, Thomas did not live long to enjoy the living for he died in office in February 1669.

THE HEARTH TAX

Charles the Second's reign was one in which the Monarch was always in need of money, and one of the schemes devised by his ministers for raising funds took the form of a tax on hearths. There were two acts, one in 1662 and one in 1664, and they called for the appointment of parish representatives, usually the borsholder or constable, to collect from residents varying amounts according to the number of hearths in their houses. This meant that some people had to pay for the privilege of owning more hearths than they had reason to use, and there was general relief when the tax was abandoned in 1689.

The records for the years 1662 and 1664 provide much information on the inhabitants of the village and of the houses in which they lived, although it is not possible to determine which houses the various families occupied. There was relaxation for those who could not afford to pay the tax, and this was based on a scale of circumstances for each householder. Anyone in receipt of poor relief or living in a house valued at less than twenty shillings a year, and so not paying parish rates, was exempt. Otherwise residents had to pay two shillings per hearth which represented quite a large outlay at that time. It was the task of the borsholder to go round the village counting the hearths and compiling lists of the householders concerned and their ability to pay. These lists had to be handed to the Justices of the Peace at the next Quarter Sessions. He then had to collect the money twice a year, at Michaelmas *(29th September)* and on Lady Day *(25th March)*.

In 1662, the borsholder was James Rallison who married Margaret Kerk on 10th December 1662. The marriage register states that he was over twenty-one years of age, and he was probably not much over that. Owing to the vagaries of spelling in those days, he appears in the register as James Rallabysonn. His list was of forty-two houses, of which only twenty-five paid the tax, the other seventeen being exempt. His own house was evidently quite small for it is mentioned as having just one hearth.

The house with the most hearths, no less than ten, was occupied by John Frembling. Two others of his family, Richard Fremblin, and Nicholas Fremblin, who were apparently in the habit of dropping their final 'g's, had two and three hearths respectively. The name has long been associated with West House, so that perhaps is where the ten hearths were. The only identified house is Dynes Farm, where John Theobald, gent. was responsible for eight hearths. Members of his family lived at Stonepitts for many years, but that house was probably listed under Seal.

Widow Miller, perhaps of the family that owned Castle Bank among other places, had to pay for five hearths, but her mother in law Widow Miller senior was not charged for her two. Maybe she was in receipt of poor relief. The Whiffens and the Christophers had large houses, each with six hearths, but it is not possible to identify them. They could be Crowdleham, Manor House at Heverham, St. Edith's Farmhouse, Ivy Farmhouse, or Noah's Ark Cottage.

Two more widows Mrs. Slidor and Mrs. Rogers had five hearths to account for as did John Allen, whose descendants lived at Yew Tree House eventually, so perhaps that is where his hearths were. Widows were plentiful in the village, for we find the names of Widows Chilmaid, Codd, Chowning, ffletcher, Mills, Haltropp and

Watts, also mentioned. Among those exempted was John ffowler, whose name appears in the marriage register of 1660 as John Foul.

Other householders not mentioned above were: one hearth, Robert Brookham; two hearths, Robert Stephens, Henry Stone, John James, Thomas Dalton, John Small, Gregory High; three hearths, William Best, Benjamin Gooden, Thomas Chilmaid; four hearths, Thomas Kipps and William Wigsell.

Those not chargeable included: one hearth, Matthias Johnson, Edward Bookham, Robert Thomas, John Williams; two hearths Thomas Pottman, John Williams senior, William French, Edmund Caldwell, Robert Charlwood and Robert Stevens senior.

It is strange that the name of the Widow Chapman does not appear anywhere in the lists, for she was the lady mentioned earlier who died in 1666 and was buried in the churchyard with head and footstones that are the oldest legible stones. There are one or two graves next to hers which could be older but they are not inscribed. It seems that she did not reside in the parish, but was brought here for burial, perhaps by relatives living here, or at her special request. Her name does not appear in any of the records, nor is the name of her husband known. The inscription on the stone reads:

"JONE CHAPMAN, WIDOW, DIED 16TH SEPTEMBER 1666".

She was probably buried in woollen because the act enforcing the use of burial shrouds of wool was passed in 1666.

DR MAXIMILIAN BUCK

It was probably just after the restoration of Charles II that the church in Kemsing was renovated and refurnished. The lower part of the screen was still in place, and a pulpit had been erected at its north end. This was a very simple affair of hexagonal shape with plain panels. The sounding board above it was also hexagonal and bore some decoration in that there were carved pendants at the angles. There was also an oak table of Jacobean design, the lower parts of which are still in use as a book table at the west end of the church, surmounted by a modern oak top. This was in all likelihood the communion table that replaced the altar in the sanctuary in Cromwellian times, when it was customary to consecrate the elements in the body of the church. In 1674 the Revd. Maximilian Buck was instituted as vicar, and it was possibly at his instigation that new pews, a western gallery for musicians and a font cover were installed. The pews were of the box type, with high walls to those at the east end, lower walls further back, and benches with no doors at the west end. Parishioners sat in these in accordance with the churchwardens' or the parish clerk's rating of their rank in the village. The western gallery was approached by a stairway against the west wall and was lit by a large window in the north wall, the two-light frame of which now holds the jumble of early glass in the north aisle . On the south side, it was unlit until the 18th century, when the present small window over the south door was inserted to give light for the musicians on that side of the gallery. The oak font cover is octagonal with a central pillar supported by flying buttresses and surmounted by an acorn. The latter may well have reference to the loyalty of the Bunce family and others in the village to the Royal family, for the oak tree was accepted as a symbol by Charles II after his escape from the Roundheads by hiding in an oak after the Battle of Worcester in 1651.

Mr. Buck was vicar for some forty-six years, during which time he resided mainly in Seal, but on August 9th 1681 he married in Kemsing church a local lady called Rebecca Hallywell. Possibly the refurnishing of the church was a preparation for this wedding. The couple evidently lived happily ever afterwards, for five years after his death in 1720 his widow gave to Seal church a splendid brass chandelier in his memory. Maximilian was the third of that name; his grandfather was a mercer in the City of London and his father held properties in Essex. Maximilian III was educated at Cambridge, and after ordination held curacies in Mapledurham, and in Hampshire, before coming to Kemsing and Seal. While here, he served as domestic chaplain to the fifth and sixth Earls and the first Duke of Dorset at Knole, where there is a picture of him as one of a group of men sitting comfortably round a table. In 1674 he gave a chalice and paten to the church at Seal. His memorial, like those of other vicars of Kemsing, is in Seal church.

LATER 17TH CENTURY

Building went on in the village all through the latter half of the 17th century. One of the houses erected was the present Vicarage, which has been estimated to date from 1680. Also the old Parsonage in St. Edith's Road was still habitable and a terrier, or inventory of the property, of 1675 shows that it held nine rooms, with three chimneys. It had three doors and ten windows, of which six had glass panes. It stood in forty rods of glebe land, bounded on the north by cottages held by John Chowning and Gregory High; on the east by the lands of Sir James Bunce and on the west by the road. Gregory High was one of the churchwardens who, with John Gransden, drew up this terrier.

Burials were still taking place within the church, and in 1675 a baby was interred in the chancel. The inscription on his grave read:

> "HERE LIETH YE BODI OF JAMES YE SON OF MILES COOKE AND ANN HIS WIFE, DAUGHTER OF JAMES BROCKMAN, ESQUIRE OF RICHBOROUGH IN KENT, AGED 12 WEEKS 4 DAYS".

The baby was probably buried in woollen, for the law enforcing this practice was still in force. Other laws were the Hearth Tax which was abolished in 1689 and the law about marking paupers and vagabonds which was still enforced up to the end of the century. Paupers had to wear a letter 'P' with the initial letter of the village in which they were living, so the borsholder, or the parish clerk, or some other worthy had to ensure that paupers in Kemsing were marked "PK".

Throughout the 17th century certain families were the leading figures in the parish. They include the Fremlins, Kipps, Wigsells, Christophers, Theobalds, Gransdens, and Highs.

There is in the church a royal coat of arms which bears the date 1721, but it is more than likely that this was originally put up over the altar at the time of the restoration of Charles II as a tribute to that monarch. In 1721 it was easily altered from CR in the corners to GR for Georgius Rex and the coat of arms in the centre re-painted. Several books were being written at that time, such as Thomas Philipotts' "Villare Cantarium", in which Kemsing Castle was described as a mess of rubbish; and Richard Kilburn's "Topographical Survey of the County of Kent". In his book, Philipott mentions a coat of arms for a family called Kemsing. Now to be seen in Lullingstone Church, it is heraldically described as: "Argent a chevron and fess interlaced sable". No reference to this family has been found elsewhere so far.

In 1698 a map now held at Maidstone shows no enclosed park for Kemsing, and the nearest road shown is the one from Seal to Riverhead.

Kemsing: Argent a chevron and fess interlaced sable

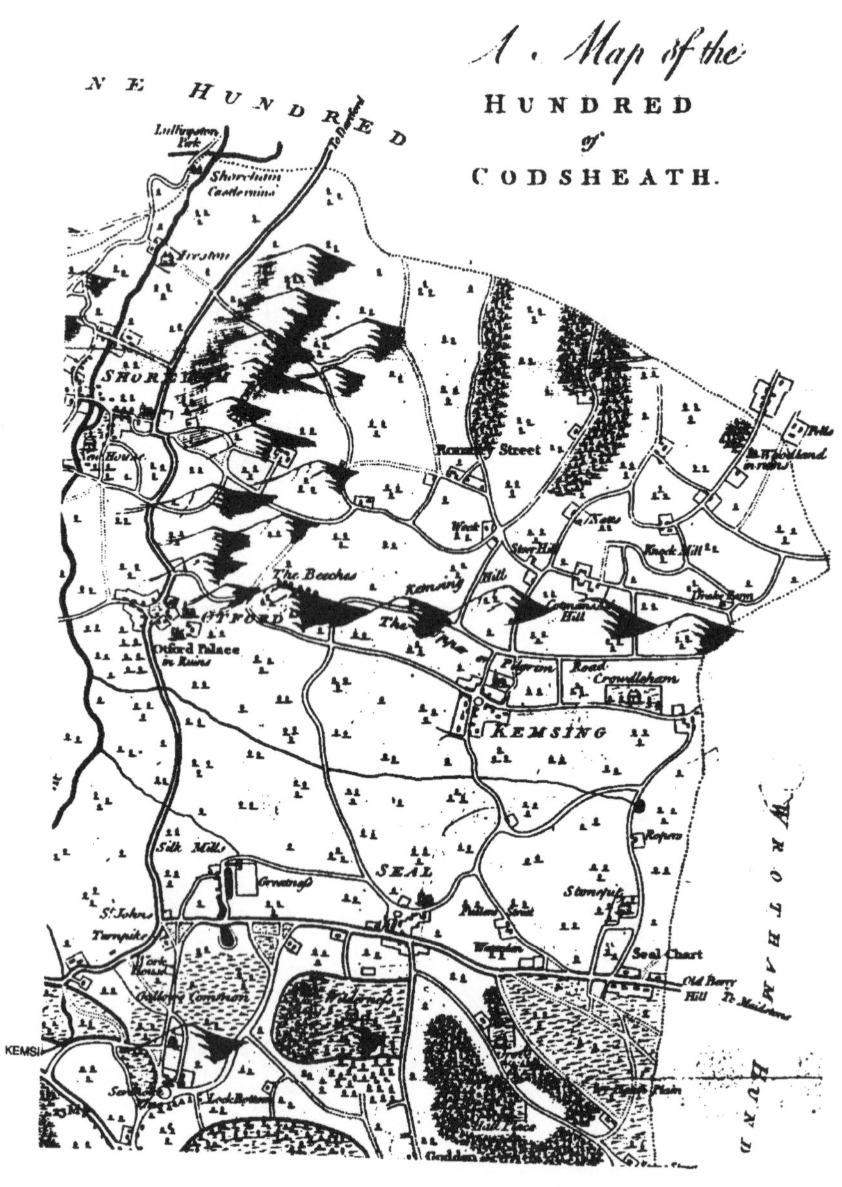

Part of the map in Hasted's 'Kent' 1784

Chapter 6
The 18th Century

Noahs Ark Cottage

The First Half

The beginning of the eighteenth century saw the erection of several new houses in Kemsing. These included Glen Cottage and Gwens Cottage which were first mentioned in a document dated 1714. Probably they were one house then and have since been divided into two. The upper floor of Gwens Cottage crosses over the second floor of Glen Cottage in what is known as a "flying freehold" and Glen Cottage has an interesting "cat-slide" roof at the rear.

Noah's Ark

Another house was Noah's Ark Cottage which was the home of Richard Christopher. His father John Christopher, who was born in Seal but died in Kemsing, was a farmer who held land in the present Noah's Ark area and at Cotmans Ash. In his will he left a field to the wife of his son Richard. Her name was Barbara French. The field was some eight acres in area in a part of Kemsing then known as Middleton Green, and it was called Hemstalle. Richard was a wheelwright and it seems that in 1703 he was negotiating with another party for a strip of land in the road between Seal and Kemsing measuring eight feet by two rods *(a rod was equivalent to five and a half yards or sixteen and a half feet)*. The interesting thing about this strip of land was that it was described as being "near to his new house, lately called Hemstall, and now called Noahs Arke".

As his father had left a field called Hemstalle, it seems that Richard had built a house on it for himself. It is not known why he chose to call it Noahs Ark. Fifteen years later Richard died, leaving his widow Barbara in possession of the house and land, on the understanding that at her death it would pass to their four sons, John, Richard, Robert and Oliver. It was quite a large house, as is shown by an inventory taken at about that time, which mentions the contents of a hall, a milkhouse, a brewhouse, a chamber over the hall, a chamber over the milkhouse, a garret and a barn. The whole property was valued at £20.8s.6d. In the event, it appears that the second son, Richard the younger, lived in the house, because when he died in 1744, he was said to have held "land at Middleton Green in Kemsing called 'Hemstalls' and also a parcel of waste".

This second Richard was also a wheelwright, which may explain why he followed his father in that house. His widow Margaret became the occupier. She had no son, but seven daughters, so the property went to a nephew, Robert the son of Oliver, who sold the property, again called "Hemstalls, alias Noahs Ark in Kemsing, also a parcel of waste there" to Benjamin Fletcher, who in turn sold to Thomas Kipps.

Queen Anne, the last of the Stuarts, was on the throne until 1714, when she was succeeded by George I of the House of Hanover. This change of dynasty marked a significant alteration in the politics of the country. Intermittent warfare on the continent meant that men from the villages were sometimes called upon to serve in the army that was led by the Duke of Marlborough to great victories over the French.

Another important political change was the union of England and Scotland in 1707 and the creation of a new national flag, the St. George's Cross being combined with the St. Andrew's

Cross to give the national colours of red, white and blue for the first time.

THE CHURCH RENOVATED

In Kemsing, the Revd. Maximilian Buck was still vicar up to 1720 when he was succeeded by Dr. Robert Parran. In 1703 Mr. Buck was involved in a local dispute. In May of that year a number of Ightham and Kemsing residents, including the churchwardens, met in a field called Lillys Meadow, to determine how much of the hay produced in that field, which lay across the boundary between the two parishes, should be allocated to the Rector of Ightham. They found that one acre only on the eastern side of the field was in Ightham parish. Among the Kemsing witnesses to the agreement drawn up were the Vicar, William Round the churchwarden, James and John Bunce, William Wigsell and John Hackett.

Dr. Parran proved to be a man sympathetic to the needs of Seal and Kemsing, but unfortunately was often more absent than present. He found Kemsing church in a sad state of repair and one of his first concerns was to make it more suitable for parish worship. He had the interior cleaned and whitened, and he caused four prayer boards to be prepared. These were to hang on either side of the east window. The two at the top contained the words of the Lord's Prayer and of the Creed, while the other two larger and lower boards held the words of the Ten Commandments. The painting of all this lettering had to be done by hand, and no doubt involved the employment of a signwriter of some experience. Although there were by this time tradesmen of most kinds in the village, it is doubtful whether a signwriter would have been found among them. For notices on shop fronts and for the painting of farm wagons a local painter would have sufficed, but for the careful painting of the prayer boards a more experienced man was probably brought in from Sevenoaks or Maidstone.

The total improvement to the church was recorded on a small

wooden board, now hanging under the tower, which reads:-

THIS CHURCH
WAS BEAUTIFIED &
THE COMMANDMENTS
& PRAYERS WERE DONE
AT YE CHARGE OF THIS
PARISH: ANNO: 1721
MR. ROBT. PARRAN, VICAR
MR. INO. CODD, CHURCHWARDEN

As already mentioned the Royal Coat of Arms was repainted and changed at about this time in honour of King George I and the House of Hanover.

Burials were still being made inside the church, and one is recorded as that of Mary Hopkins who was buried in the chancel. Her grave was inscribed

"HERE LYETH THE BODE OF MARY HOPKINS, SISTER TO GEORGE SCELLEY, BART WHO DIED THE 12 OF OCTOBER 1722 AGE 29 YEARS".

In the churchyard more and more stone memorials were being erected including those of several of the Wigsell family from 1669 to 1738; the Kipps family from 1721 to 1728; and the Hackett family from 1721 to 1739. These stones are all well preserved and are good examples of the changes of monumental design from the plain and somewhat gloomy aspect of death represented by skulls and crossed bones etc to the more enlightened vision of death and the afterlife, represented by such devices as rays of light and winged cherubs.

Roads throughout the country were being developed as the need arose for the accommodation of more and more traffic, and a milestone was put up at the junction of Childsbridge Lane and the Pilgrims Way, to mark the distances in each direction. These were: To Malling 10 miles, to Bromley 12 miles, to Dartford 12 miles, and to Sevenoaks 5 miles. This was an important crossroads, marking the meeting point of the west to east road, i.e. the Pilgrims Way, and the north to south road from Dartford to Tonbridge.

Three arms of this crossroads are still in constant use, but the fourth has declined into a mere bridleway known locally these days as Chalky Lane.

In 1703 there occurred a great storm, comparable with that experienced in the south of England in October 1987, which devastated large tracts of the country. It overturned the lighthouse newly erected by the architect Winstanley at Eddistone. Parts of the national fleet were sunk off the Goodwin Sands. Kemsing must have suffered the loss of many trees and perhaps much damage to buildings but there is no record of this.

A terrier or inventory was made of the Parsonage house in 1726. This building stood in St. Edith's Road and the terrier shows that it had recently been converted into two dwellings of six bays in all, and it stood in fifteen rods of glebe land. Changes in the naming of houses are exemplified by the new name of Monks in the Hole, which now became Haltrops Bottom, because the Haltrop family had moved in. The present vicarage was called Wallis House after the Wallis family, Richard and his wife Anne with several of their children.

Crime was not noticeably prevalent in the village. An article in the General Evening Post for 30th September 1738 recorded a robbery from Kemsing church on 16th of that month. It talks about a band of sacrilegious rogues infesting the Sevenoaks district, breaking into and robbing most of the churches around. From Kemsing they stole a blue velvet pulpit cover with a gold border, a cushion of velvet and a communion table cloth.

LATE 18TH CENTURY

The new vicar appointed after the death of Dr. Parran in 1739 was the Revd. Thomas Curteis, who resigned the living after just over four years to become the Rector of Sevenoaks. His successor was the Revd. Gregory Sharpe who was already Vicar of Birling. He again did not stay long and went on to hold many important posts in the church and became the author of several religious books;

he was also the Master of the Temple, and Director of the Society of Antiquaries of London.

The curate at this time, the Revd. Carswell Winder, had entered the church on the advice of his friends, who thought it would sober him down from his customary mode of living which included hunting. In fact he became known as one of the hunting parsons of that age.

After twenty-eight years as curate, enjoying a stipend of some £35 per annum, he became Rector of Halstead, but continued as curate of Kemsing until 1761, when he was instituted as Vicar. To enable him to run both parishes, he appointed his youngest brother, William Winder as curate at Halstead in 1758 and at Kemsing in 1759.

On the death of Mr. Winder in 1770, the Revd. William Humphrey was instituted as Vicar. He also held the living of Birling from 1782 and remained Vicar of Kemsing for forty-six years, almost as long as had the Revd. Maximilian Buck.

For information on what went on in the village, the churchwardens' accounts make it possible to follow some of the advances made in the standard of living of the villagers, and also outline some of the trials and tribulations that they had to endure. Among the latter was the effect of a great storm on 19th August 1763, when a strip of land between Tunbridge Wells and Sheerness was devastated. Hailstones of reputedly nine inches across fell in Maidstone. No mention is made of Kemsing, but there was probably some damage to crops, etc.

Another year, 1795, saw much cold weather when the whole district was covered in snow and ice and the Medway was frozen over.

A further trial was the introduction in 1783 of a tax of threepence levelled on every entry in the parish registers. As a result, some of the records of baptisms, marriages and burials of the poorest inhabitants were not registered or, if they were, they had the indignity of having the word "poor" written against the entry. Fortunately this tax was removed in 1795.

Some consternation may have been caused in the village when

the Gregorian Calendar was introduced in place of the Julian to bring England into line with other European countries. This meant that, on September 3rd 1752, the dates 3rd to 13th September were "lost", and thereafter the year began on 1st January instead of 25th March. In some places there were demonstrations by people demanding their eleven days back but no record exists of what the Kemsing residents felt.

Builders were busy erecting new houses and altering old ones. At St. Clere, Mr. William Evelyn made extensive alterations in 1767, and in 1759 Ivy Cottage in Watery Lane was either built or renovated. A tablet over the door bears the initials "R.W" and the date. As there were some fourteen male persons alive in Kemsing at that time bearing the initials "R.W" it is not possible to be sure who the builder was.

FIRST NATIONAL CENSUS

Soon after the close of the eighteenth century, the first national census return in 1801 records that there were sixty-one houses inhabited by three-hundred and twenty people. In the next ten years, this number had become sixty-six houses occupied by three-hundred and sixteen people. A rough look at the village houses as they are today indicates that the first sixty-one existing in 1801 included the following:- At Heverham, Nearly Corner, Letter Box House, Ivy Cottage, The Chequers, Walnut Tree Cottage and its annexe, the three Forge Cottages and Broughton. At Crowdleham, there was Crowdleham House and Crowdleham Farmhouse, and the two Plum Tree Cottages and the Malthouse. In the village were Old Wybournes, the two Wybournes Cottages, to which were attached the five old Post Office Cottages, Glen Cottage and Gwens Cottage, Yew Tree House, Foster House, the butchers shop, The Bell, and 1 and 3 St. Edith's Road. In St. Edith's Road were two Parsonage Cottages, St. Edith's Farmhouse, Dynes Farmhouse and cottages and Noahs Ark Cottage. Also in the village were Wallis House *(the Vicarage)*, the Wheatsheaf, Well Cottage, Rose

Cottage, two in The Keep, three in Castle Bank, three in Sunny Bank where Nutshell Cottage is now, West House, Ivy Farm House and Cottage, and numbers 47 and 49 West End. Outside the village were Dippers Hall, Stub Crouch *(now Chart Rise)*, the Mud Hut *(now Childs Cottage)*, Shorehill Cottage, Cold Bank, and the two St. Edith's Cottages. With a possible extra Plum Tree Cottage and a now demolished dwelling in front of Wybournes Cottages, the total of sixty-one is reached.

Beside the building of houses, roads were being improved, and a new one now called Polhill, was built to replace part of the old London Road through Knockholt. Milestones were set up along the new turnpike roads. In Kemsing men were employed to knap flints, which were kept in piles ready for use to repair potholes.

Repairs were continually being made to the Church. These involved such items as painting the tower and steeple white, constant re-tiling of the roof, and repainting the letters on the prayer boards inside the church. In 1772 two-thousand, five hundred roof tiles were supplied by Stephen Porter, who provided a further thousand three years later. Windows were mended by Charles Rogers in 1777, and the next year five shillings were spent on illuminating the church: and work was done on the church spire: the letters on the prayer boards were painted over by John Kipps, who charged £5.12s.3d for seventy-two dozen letters. Lead for mixing the paint was sold by Richard Harvey. Further work on the church fabric, involving brick laying and window glazing, was undertaken in 1792; and in 1798 timber and boards costing over twenty-seven pounds were needed to repair the tower and spire. This last work was done by John Corke of Seal. The bell ropes appear to have worn out frequently and new ones were bought if the old ones could not be repaired by John Covell.

This sort of information is obtained from the churchwardens accounts of which only those written between 1767 and 1843 are available. The churchwardens involved at this time included Richard Kipps, Robert Relph, John Turner, Thomas Palmer, John Wigsell, Thomas Taylor, John Bennett, Thomas Relph, Thomas Bennett and another Thomas Relph. These men were responsible for caring for the poor and needy and some of their expenses were incurred while doing this sort of work. For instance, in 1782, the churchwarden was obliged to find a midwife to attend the confinement of one Phyllis Cambery, who was too poor to arrange this for herself. Moreover, the only midwife available had to be fetched on horseback.

SMUGGLING

Like many another village in North West Kent, Kemsing had a claim to have been involved in the smuggling of contraband goods from the Kent coast to London in the late 18th and early 19th centuries. There is no written evidence that Kemsing men participated in these activities, except for one entry in the Burial Register. This states that on the 16th of February, 1776, John Wells of the parish of Smarden, aged thirty-seven was buried in the churchyard, having been shot by an Excise man of Sevenoaks while smuggling goods through Kemsing. He is not likely to have been doing this without the connivance of some of the villagers. Apart from this there is nothing but hearsay about such things as a smugglers field, the use of the cellar of Clement House for storage and odd goings on in Noah's Ark Cottage. It has also been suggested that the Wigsell family of Kemsing were active in smuggling. As far as the cellar of Clement House is concerned, that must have been a house on the site upon which Clement House itself was built in 1865 when smuggling activities had ceased.

But that smuggling certainly went on in the area is demonstrated by the story written in 1888 by John Terry, of Platt Grange, Wrotham Common. He was a member of a wool business with offices in the City of London, who had a country house at Old Terry's Lodge, Wrotham. Close by was a beacon guarded by soldiers at the time of the Napoleonic Wars, and this was a great nuisance to the smugglers *(known as Free Traders)*, who also had a signalling post on the hillside. This took the form of a large field on which domestic animals such as cows and horses were tethered in certain recognisable formations known to the smugglers which indicated the presence, approach or general whereabouts of the Revenue Officers. Guards of the coaches that ran several times a day from Canterbury to London also helped the smugglers, who could tell by the tunes played on the coachman's horns just where the preventive men were on the road to the coast. Another group involved were the birch broom makers, who worked in the woods at Wrotham Heath. When they took their wares to London for sale they often covered barrels of brandy with birch brooms. Sometimes smaller amounts of illicit goods were brought up from places such as Sandwich and Hythe by dogcart to Wrotham where they were transferred to horses which took the goods to London. These dogcarts were pulled by two dogs, one from Wrotham and the other from the coastal town concerned, so that whichever way they travelled one dog knew the way home. Small boys were often sent on these errands. Other deliveries were made in bulk and as many as two hundred horses could be used for one consignment.

So there is not much doubt that Kemsing men would have joined in on such occasions. The penalties for breaking the law were severe, and men from the villages were often ruined if they were caught. The organisers of the trade however, being rich London businessmen, were not worried. If caught they could afford the fine, however heavy, but if they got away with it the financial gains were very considerable. Whether there were hiding places in Kemsing or not, there certainly were some at Oldbury Hill, at the Sand Quarry at St. Mary Platt, and Gallows Hill, near the Windmill on Wrotham Heath. A field to the east of Cockney's Wood, shown on the Tithe Map of 1840, is called Wiggals Barn. Was this a corruption of Wigzel's Barn and was that another hiding place? And one other speculation - in 1830 Henry Bowyer of Kemsing married Jane Ransley. Was she a connection of George Ransley, a smuggler from Aldington Frith on Romney Marsh who was caught and deported to Tasmania in 1826?

Trades And Occupations

While the village had always been well served by its tradesmen, not much is known about them until the end of the 18th century, when entries in the churchwardens' accounts reveal not only the names of these men but also their trades. Farming was the main occupation of the parish, and here everything was dependent on the horse, so those who dealt with horses were numerous - blacksmiths to shoe them, wheelwrights to provide cartwheels, carpenters to make the carts, ostlers and grooms to care for the animals, stable boys to clean the stables and the farmyards, tanners to make leather for the saddlers and shoemakers to work on. For housing, there were bricklayers, carpenters, joiners, thatchers, and glaziers.

Clothing was supplied by tailors, women knitters and needlewomen, and food provision came from the butcher, the baker, the gardener, hop grower and brewer.

Among such tradespeople mentioned in the accounts were William How, cordwainer *(shoemaker)*; Richard Wallis, tailor, William Knell, wheelwright; Richard Kipps, builder and decorator; Robert Bookham, husbandman; John Kipps, painter; Richard Harvey, shopkeeper; Thomas Relph, tilemaker; Mr.Gilberd, builder; Thomas Taylor, farmer; and William Eve, shopkeeper.

The parish clerk held an important position in the village. In church his duty was to lead the congregation in the responses and to lead the singing of the psalms by the psalm singers in the west gallery. The churchwardens' duties often took them out of the parish to consult lawyers, buy registry books and so on. They had to come to the rescue of helpless people such as Phyllis Cambery, mentioned earlier, Thomas Kipps being the churchwarden involved. When William Wynn was parish clerk, he set up a dial post and painted it himself, while John Kipps put the dial on it. Presumably this was some sort of sun-dial. Where it stood is not known, but it was probably in the churchyard.

This was the period of the Napoleonic Wars, and men of serviceable age were liable to be called up on duty with the militia. Instances of this are recorded as follows: 1803, one man named

William Roots was selected by ballot to represent Kemsing, and he was given time to find a substitute if he so wished. 1805, two men had to be found by either Seal or Kemsing. In 1806, nine men over the age of thirty were needed from Kemsing, together with one man who had no children, and four men who had children under the age of fourteen. There were six exemptions at this time, for five yeomen or volunteers and one of the following: clergyman, trader, medicine man or constable.

There were at least two inns in the village at the end of the 18th century. The Bell is mentioned in a list of Kentish Public houses dated 1750. The publican was John Kipps. Another name was The Swann, and this may well have referred to the forerunner of to-day's Wheatsheaf. The publican there was William Elcombe.

THE FREMLIN FAMILY

FREMLIN

From 1561 to 1813 the parish registers contain no fewer than forty-seven references to the Fremlin family, the last being the burial on 10th October 1793 of John Fremlin, aged seventy-six. He was a pauper, and as there are no further references to the family it must be concluded that the more affluent members had by that time moved away from Kemsing. Their descendants are now living in many parts of the world, including members of the Kentish brewing family. In 1992 a party of sixteen of them, coming from Kent, Essex, Canada and New Zealand visited Kemsing.

William the Conqueror appointed his half-brother Odo, Bishop of Bayeux, to be Earl of Kent, and the Domesday Book shows that one Godfrey de Ros held "La Sela" under the new earl. While he may not have lived in the area, it has been claimed that another of the earl's supporters, called Mellin, settled in Kemsing in A.D. 1068. As he was a Norman the Saxon villagers called him Fra Mellin, the Fra meaning "stranger". This appellation was modified as time went on to Framellin and Fremellin. It was rendered in various different ways until finally becoming Fremlin, and the descendants of Fra Mellin became the ancestors of a family that inhabited Kemsing for some seven or eight hundred years.

Although this legend must be regarded as fanciful it is perhaps possible that the name Fremlin is derived from the word "fremman", meaning stranger or foreigner. Or again, it has been claimed by an Australian member of the family that it is derived from a Dutch word "vrijmolen" *(free mill)*, through a French version "Fremoulin" to an Anglicised Fremolyn, Fremling, etc. Whatever the truth of the Fra Mellin story it is known that Fremlins were undoubtedly living in the parish in the thirteenth century, because in 1275 Rulfus Fremolin and Michel ffremolin with ten others served on a jury at a trial held in Kemsing. *(The double small ff was the equivalent of the modern capital F.)*. In the fourteenth century Robert Fremellyn sold a rod of land in 1339 to the Rector, the Revd. Gilbertus de Kekeshill. In the following century John Fremlyn, by his will made in 1457, left a sheep to the shrine of St. Edith. Two years later Walter Fremlyn left seven candles to be burnt in the church and chapel, while William Fremlyn asked to be buried in the churchyard.

A very interesting record serves to connect the sixteenth century with the twentieth, in that on the tenth of January 1515 Raynold Fremlyn bequeathed to William and John Fremlyn two pieces of land, one called Crokyn Pittes and the other Kokney Wood. The latter, now known as Cockneys or Cockness Wood, must be a very ancient piece of woodland.

One of the churchwardens in 1634 was James Fremlyn, who with his fellow warden John Gransden, drew up a terrier of the glebelands in the parish. On the sixth of November 1643 Cockneys Wood was again mentioned, this time being bequeathed by William Fremlyn to his brother George. The next year William

Fremlyn died leaving eighty-six acres of land, possibly including the same Cockneys Wood.

Two other fields were left by John Fremlyn the Elder in his will dated 20th July 1668 to his wife Anne. They were called Hills Mead and Beans Croft.

During the Commonweath Nicholas Fremlyn was appointed to be "Parish Clark" and Register". As the latter he had to enter particulars of baptisms, marriages and burials in the parish registers. Two of these entries, in 1655 and 1656, mention the fact that he was a tailor.

Chapter 7
The Early 19th Century

Vicars, Curates And Tradesmen

During the first half of the nineteenth century there were four vicars of Kemsing and Seal. The Revd. William Humphrey had already held the living for thirty years when the century began, and he was destined to remain vicar for another sixteen years. The Revd. Gervas Whitehead died in 1838 after sixteen years in office: the Revd. John Netherton Harward remained here until his resignation in 1846: and the Revd. Thomas Offspring Blackall had begun a long period as vicar.

The Revd. William Humphrey was a cultured man, a great botanist and a poet, who was also very fond of gardening. He had a brother Ozias, who was a portrait painter of some note. William's wife, Elizabeth came from the Woodgate family, who were very influential in West Kent. They had two sons, William Ozias and George, who both died young, but their daughters survived. Mr. Humphrey's churchwardens during the last sixteen years of his office were: John Wigsell, Thomas Taylor, John Turner, John Marvin, John Bennett, Thomas Relph, Junior, Thomas Relph, Senior and Thomas Bennett.

He completed nearly forty-six years as vicar, most of which time he devoted to Seal, and when he died on 19th July 1816, he was buried at Seal. His widow survived him by eighteen years. She resided in Seal, but had an interest in Kemsing in that she was the owner of Noah's Ark. A plan dated 1828, signed John Cronk, shows that this property consisted of a house and just over seven acres of land, divided into four fields, called The House Meadow, Hither Meadow, Middle Meadow and Further Meadow. This corresponds closely with the land called Hemstall that John Christopher owned in the late seventeenth century and on which his son Richard built the house called Noah's Ark. Mrs. Humphrey received £3.15s.6d a year rent for "Akehurst's Cottage" at Noah's Ark. This must have been Noah's Ark Cottage, evidently occupied by one Mr. Akehurst, but in 1839 when the Tithe Map was surveyed the whole property was owned by Frances Humphrey (presumably a daughter as Mrs. Humphrey had died in 1835 aged eighty-four). Frances let part of the house to John Russell while the other half was empty. The four fields were let to Amos Swaisland who farmed St. Edith's Farm. The next vicar, the Revd. Gervas Whitehead, was a great friend of the Humphreys, and at one time it was felt he might marry their daughter Juliana. He had been Master of the Sevenoaks Grammar School for twenty-four years up to 1813. He was also the vicar of All Saints, Cambridge. Owing to the unfitness of the Glebe House in Kemsing, he obtained permission from the Bishop of Rochester to reside in Seal. This is somewhat odd, because the Glebe or Parsonage House had not been used by the clergy for many years. Mr. Whitehead served as vicar for twenty-two years. He was a classical scholar as is mentioned on the mural tablet to his memory in Seal church. He died in 1838.

During his time there were curates looking after Kemsing. From time to time they included Henry Hatch, H.J. Wharton, Henry Engleheart, and William Stamer. These four took most of the services at Kemsing. On the death of Mr. Whitehead, the Revd. John Netherton Harward was appointed as vicar. He came with a wife and eight children and after his eight years in the parish he left with a round dozen. He lived at Oak Bank in Grove Road, Seal, which was said by some of his neighbours to be far too grand for a vicar. His story properly belongs to Seal as he took all the services and offices there, leaving curates to look after Kemsing. These young men were Essex Holcombe, Francis Cooke, H. Johnson Marshall, Edward Bayliss, and T.O. Blackall. They were required to live within half a mile of Kemsing church, and as the Glebe House was still not available they had to find lodgings in the village. They were poorly paid, and this perhaps accounts for the quick changeover.

When he resigned Mr. Harward went to East Grinstead, and died there in 1863. Besides being vicar of Kemsing and Seal, he was for some years domestic chaplain to the Bishop of Rochester. During his last year here, the Malling Deanery which included Kemsing and Seal was transferred from Rochester Diocese to Canterbury, where it remained until 1905. The vicar's only possession in Kemsing was the Glebe House or Parsonage in St Edith's Road, which was in 1841 let to James Whiffen and a Mr. Laws.

It was in this period that the churchwardens' accounts provided more information about the village and its inhabitants. It is possible to glean from them many names of local personalities, most of whom were involved in some way with supplying the church with goods or services. They make it possible to determine the trades and professions applicable to some of the men who rejoiced in the same name; for instance, there were three men called George Kipps. One was a painter, one was an agricultural labourer, and the third was a builder. It is interesting to note from several references to repairs of bell ropes in the church that inflation was rampant during the first twenty years of the century. In 1800, James Atherfold was paid sixteen shillings to repair the ropes. In 1803, the cost was 18s.8d. In 1805, 19s. In 1807, £1.6s.0d. In 1809, £1.4s.9d. and in 1811, £1.8s 6d. This represents an inflation rate of about 80% in some ten years and reflects the fact that the country was involved in the Napoleonic Wars and that rope was very much in demand by the Navy.

The church was in continual need of repair. Such items as timber, being needed for repairing not only the building but the fences round it, had to come from John Cork at Seal, and many journeys were made over the next few years. Sand and lime and tiles also had to be collected, the latter coming from Wrotham, supplied by Mr. Skinner, who charged six pounds for three thousand tiles. John Kipps was always available for small repairs not only to the church but also to its contents, such as the pulpit and the coffin bier. Bricklaying was done by Mr. Smith and windows were repaired by a man called Booth. It was also John Kipps who repaired the church dial, and painted the outside of the church. Trees in the churchyard had to be pollarded and this was done by Thomas Thorpe.

The bells themselves were sometimes in need of repair. One developed a split in the bottom which was healed by drilling a round hole at the top of the crack.

Wine for the communion service was supplied by Mrs. Atherfold, who apparently kept a shop in the village, and prayer books had to be fetched from Maidstone and were continuously being replaced. The music in church was supplied by the Psalm Singers sitting in the west gallery, and the churchwardens were responsible for their pay and for giving them an annual feast.

At the beginning of the century there were sixty-one houses, and the census returns at ten-year intervals indicate that the numbers were increased by five up to 1811, four more up to 1821, two more in 1831, and a further two in 1841.

Various other events of some note took place during this period. An accident occurred in 1824 when on 24th July the Parish Clerk, one William Hook, was killed while working in the Chalk Pit, but which chalk pit is not known.

In 1826 the remaining fourteenth and fifteenth century glass is said to have been removed by the churchwardens in spite of a protest made by the vicar, Mr. Whitehead. The jumble of glass now in the north aisle indicates that these windows included the old east window in which was a representation of the Crucifixion.

The bridge over the Guzzle Brook in Childsbridge Lane being in need of repair at that time, it was arranged that the expense should be shared by the parishes of Kemsing and Seal. There was debate in 1847 about the road from Kemsing to Heverham. A proposition that it should be repaired and widened was turned down by the churchwardens and the way warden.

In 1816, life was pretty miserable because there was virtually no summer, as an earthquake centred in the East Indies had sent volcanic dust around the world, blocking out the sun for months. Another unfortunate year was endured in 1846, when, because of the failure of crops, and particularly of the potato crop, there was famine in Ireland and distress in many parts of England.

Oast Houses, which had now become familiar in the country, were first built in Kemsing in the year 1835, but which these were is not clear.

In 1825, there was an amusing incident when a French hot air balloon descended on a field on Seal Chart. Local voluntary help was called for to rescue the crew and get the balloon afloat again, and men from Kemsing were called upon. They apparently did not behave themselves as well as was desired by the gentry of Seal, and Mr. Round of Stonepitts declared "that these men were the greatest rascals in all Kent". It is of note that the men of nineteenth-century Kemsing were frequently referred to as being rough and ill-mannered.

THE TITHE MAP

Tithes had been paid over the centuries in keeping with the biblical concept that one tenth of a man's goods should be devoted to the service of God. By the time of the Norman Conquest a fairly well organised way of collecting and distributing these tithes had been devised. Payment was made in kind and was initially intended for the upkeep of the parish churches and priests. During the Middle Ages both the Church and the wealthy magnates built churches throughout the land, and those in Kent were sufficient in number to service the people of the county right up to the nineteenth century. Priests were appointed to look after the congregations of these churches, either by the Bishop, if he or some church authority had built the church, or by the Lord of the Manor if he had done so. There was often some doubt as to who was ultimately responsible for the parish priest's welfare and guidance. If a local lord, or seigneur, built a church for the people in his domain he was not allowed to use it later for any other purpose or to pull it down. Likewise if he appointed a priest he could not dismiss him without the Bishop's permission. A certain area of land had to be set aside as "Glebe Land" for the maintenance of the parson. But this was not sufficient to keep him and tithes were imposed to augment the living. These were divided into Great Tithes and Small Tithes. The Great Tithe was a tenth of the more important crops like wheat and corn, while the Small Tithes were derived from smaller items such as poultry and lambs. To store these payments of goods in kind, barns were built. Many, of the larger ones still standing are known as Tithe Barns. More often than not the Great Tithe was appropriated by the Lord of the Manor, while the priest had to divide the Small Tithe into four parts - for the upkeep of the church building, for the Bishop, for the sick and poor and for himself. He was usually very much the servant of the Lord of the Manor although at the same time having to be obedient to his Diocesan Bishop. The Great Tithe began to be a saleable asset and was sold as a whole or in parts, with the result that the living was often held by several people or bodies, many of them nowhere near to the parish in question. A parish was defined by taking in the boundaries of all the fields that contributed to the tithe for a particular priest. They did not always comprise a single large area, and in the case of Kemsing there were fifty acres separated from the main parish, known as Kemsing Without, which now form part of the parish of Ash.

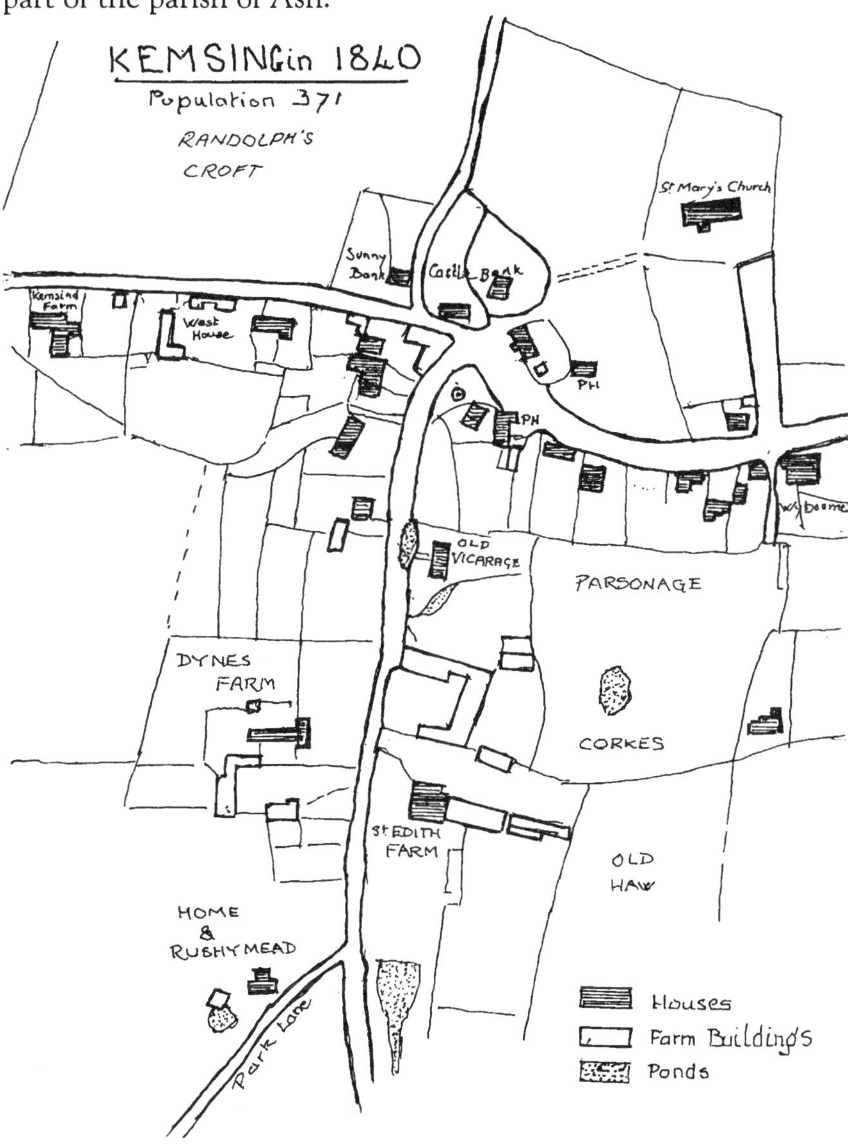

As time went on payment of tithes in kind became more and more difficult to maintain and sometimes arrangements were made, illegally, for payment in cash to be substituted. This led to great confusion and in the early nineteenth century Parliament set about reforming the situation. After one or two unsuccessful attempts the Tithe Commutation Act was passed in 1836. This called for a complete survey of all the parishes in the land, amounting to something equivalent to the Domesday survey and preceding large-scale Ordnance Survey mapping in this area. Parishes were required to produce a map showing every field and open space such as roads and waste areas, and a book was to be compiled in which these areas could be fully described as to area *(in acres, and/or roods)*, ownership, occupation, state of cultivation and local names. This book was then to be submitted to the Tithe Commissioners who would value each area and determine the amount of money due to be paid in lieu of tithes.

In the case of Kemsing Parish two maps had to be made and two books compiled, because it included Seal, Underriver, Godden Green and Stone Street. As these places were all served by the Seal Church, with its own churchwardens, parish clerk, overseers, etc. it had to have its own map, which left Kemsing village with Heverham and Noah's Ark in a much smaller area. The surveyor employed was William Cronk of Fuller Street, Seal, and his assistant was his son John. They had the task of traversing every field and space in the parish, measuring and recording details. The task was started in 1839 and not finally approved by the Tithe Commissioners until 1841. There was some movement of population during those two years, but by comparing the information provided by the map and the apportionment book with the details given in the national census return made in 1841 it is possible to form a good overall picture of what the village was like at that time.

Life in Kemsing went at the pace of a working horse. Living conditions were not good. Roads and communications were poor, water had to come from the wells, food was unvaried and expensive, there was no regular school. Most of the men were agricultural labourers, having to do every sort of job that was required in farming. Some of the women were domestic servants in the farmers' houses. There were a few each of the necessary tradesmen such as carpenters, blacksmiths, wheelwrights, sawyers, publicans, butchers, bakers, tailors and so on. But there were no "gentry" to look after the needs of the people, most of the landowners being "outlanders". In particular there was no resident vicar, for as we have seen, the Revd. John N. Harward lived at Oakbank, in Seal, and left the care of Kemsing church to curates.

From the Tithe Map we can make a complete list of the field names as they stood in 1839. Fields had to be named in order that they could be identified. The late Mr. Gershom Williams related how, as a boy in the 1890s, he was sometimes sent with messages to farmers or their labourers and he was always told that they would be found in such and such a field. He knew the names of every field in Kemsing and needed no further direction, although names did change from time to time as owners or occupiers changed. Not only owners gave their names to fields, but topographical features, such as Long Downs, which was the name given to that strip of land on the south slope of the Downs, north of the Pilgrims Way between what is now the Common Field and Cotmans Ash crossroads; Bridge Mead which was next to the bridge over the Guzzle Brook in Childsbridge Lane; Crossway Field which was on the corner of the crossroads again at Cotmans Ash Lane; and Hopgarden Field, because it was used as such. Among those named after people were Beaumonts Meadow, Benjamins Land, Austens Field, Hacketts Mead, Derries Shaw, Bakers Mead, Tanners Land, Amherst Mead, Palmers Mead, Farrants Mead, Larkin Mead, Lillies Field, Allen Field, Colemans Arable, Medhurst Bank, Burgess Shaw and Assisters Island.

Descriptive names included: Three Corner Mead, Kitchen Croft, Kiln Field, Landway Field, Bell Inn Yard, Broad Piece, Stub Crouch *(this could possibly refer to the fact that it included the base or remains of a wayside cross)*, Banky Field, Thistley Field, Cowlodge Meadow, Pond Field, Bushey Field, Fox Hills, Flaxen Mead, Timber Wood, Stock Field, Barnyard Orchard, Cricketing Field, Church Field,

Cold Banks, Walnut Tree Field, Willow Piece, White Field, Furze Field, Broom Field, Bottom Field, Green Hill and Side Hill, Badgers Mount, Rough Downs, and Barn Field.

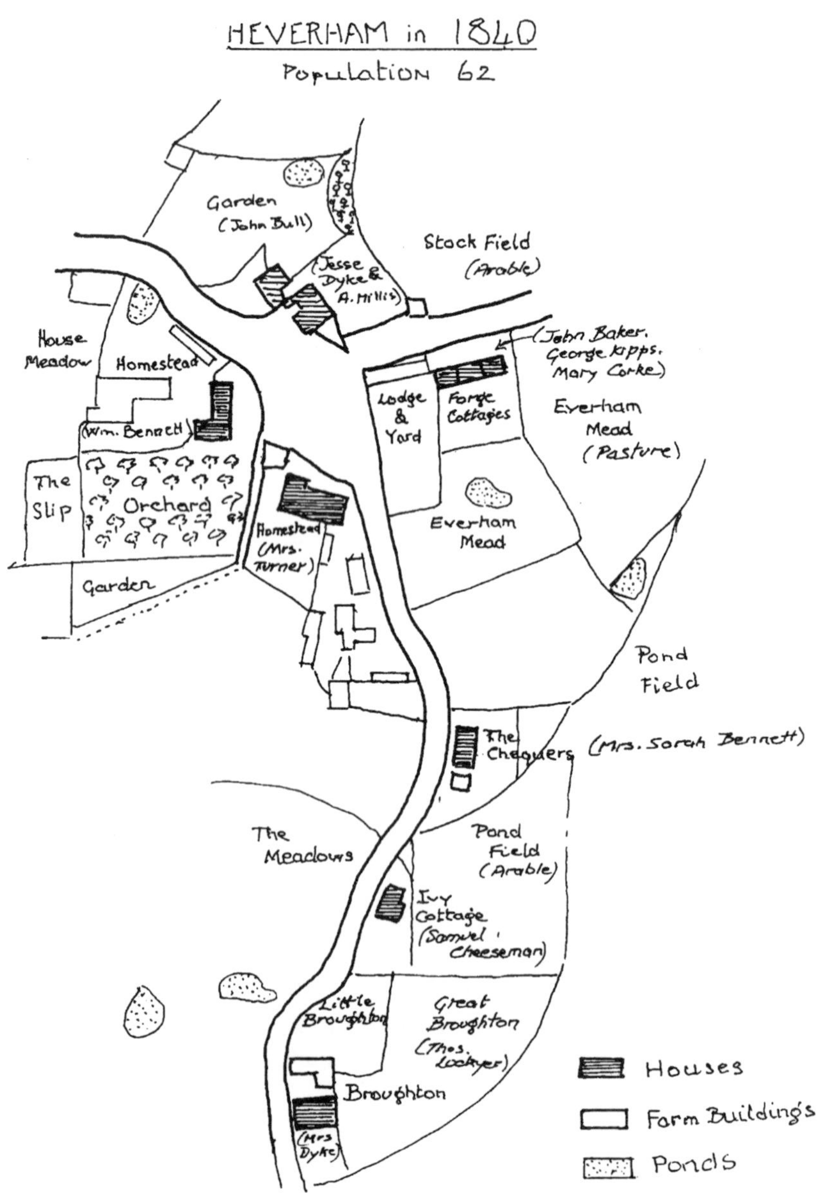

Some of the unusual names defy explanation, such as: Knaves Corner Shaw, Christmas Bush, Mag Bowles, Wiggles Barn, and Beede Mead.

In the years that have passed, many of these names have been changed but some are still retained, often in the names given to new roads, and housing developments, and private houses. Among these are Fairfield, which is now Fairfield Close; and Kester in which is the house called Kester.

The parish of Kemsing formed a jigsaw puzzle of nearly four hundred fields owned and occupied by a great number of different people. The Tithe Map reveals that some sixty per cent of the parish was held by eight landowners, most of whom were non-resident. The remainder was owned in small parcels by local people, many of whom worked their smallholdings as farms. The owner of about one quarter of the parish, some four hundred acres, was William Guest. His land ran north to south in the centre of the parish from the top of the downs to Noah's Ark. It was farmed for him by Amos Swaisland, who lived in St. Edith's Farmhouse. Nearly three hundred acres were held by the Revd. Archdeacon Edward Berens of Shrivenham in Wiltshire. They lay mostly at Heverham, spreading across the downs towards Wrotham, and were farmed mostly by Mrs. Elizabeth Turner and her son George, but also in a smaller way by William Bennett.

The next in size with one hundred and sixty acres was Dynes Farm, lying between St. Edith's Road and the Otford border south of the Pilgrims Way. Mr.Charles Willard farmed it himself, but as he was secretary to Sevenoaks School he lived in Sevenoaks and let Dynes Farmhouse to a Mr. William Pink. The Trustees of Richard Cooper owned one hundred and fifty acres, including the Landway and land stretching northwards up to the top of the downs. The farmer was Thomas Burgess, and he lived in Ivy Farm House, which was then called Kemsing Farm. Philip Firmin of Crowdleham owned one hundred and forty four acres, including Crowdleham and the land southwards from the Pilgrims Way as far as the Guzzle Brook. This was also farmed by Thomas Burgess.

The next three owners with just over one hundred acres each

were the Trustees of Stephen Grantham, for whom James Selby of Seal farmed on the Otford border; the executors of George Polhill, represented by Mr. Hiorns, farmed land towards Otford north of the Pilgrims Way. They also managed the forty-eight acres of Row Dow Wood themselves. The Trustees of William Evelyn of St. Clere held much of Ightham parish, and one hundred and two acres lying within the Kemsing boundary. This was farmed by Thomas Lockyer, who lived at Lower St. Clere.

The concept of the neighbourhood watch is not new - it was first evidenced in this area in the year 1840, when a number of residents of the parishes of Sevenoaks, Seal, Kemsing, Otford, Sundridge, Chevening and Brasted, formed a society "for the protection of property and prosecution of thieves and other criminal offenders". Some of the landholders of Kemsing may have joined this society. Members held annual meetings on 29th November each year at the Crown Inn, Sevenoaks, when twelve were elected as a committee to manage the affairs of the society. The admission fee was fourpence in the pound on the amount at which their property was rated in the poor books. A list of rewards for apprehension of offenders ran from £50 for a murderer, through £20 for a housebreaker, highwayman, footpad, horse-stealer or arsonist, to £10 for a thief of a whole list of things, including animals, and £2 for a thief who stole smaller items like ducks, wood, or implements of husbandry.

The 1841 Census Return

Although national census returns had been made in the years 1801, 1811, 1821 and 1831, the information they gave was of so little value that they were not made available. Thus it is not until 1841 that all the four-hundred and thirty-three inhabitants of Kemsing were listed, and their occupations shown. Ages were shown to the nearest multiple of five, and the place of birth was not given, apart from a note if they were not born in Kent. The enumerator was George Masters, and he started his tour of the village on 12th

June 1841, completing it by 16th. Addresses were not recorded, making it difficult to determine who lived where. Cottages were often crowded, holding parents, grandparents, children and lodgers. Only ten people were described as being of independent means, whilst seven were labelled as paupers.

Some of the women were shown as servants. Many others worked occasionally as nurses or sempstresses etc. and all had to help on the land at harvest time. The men were mostly agricultural labourers. There were seventy-four in all working for nine different farmers.

Tradesmen included three shoemakers, four wheelwrights, two blacksmiths, one beer seller, three tailors, one umbrella maker, three sawyers, two thatchers, one collier, one gamekeeper, and one bricklayer. For the sale of food and goods, there were a fishmonger, a grocer, two publicans, and a dealer.

Listed among all these and responsible for their spiritual welfare was just one clergyman, the Revd. Henry Johnson Marshall, the curate, who lodged at West House.

Unlike present day farming with its large areas of land devoted to single crops, the parish of Kemsing in 1841 was made up of small areas of very different types. Most of the fields were given over to arable, or ploughland, while a little was devoted to meadowland for cattle raising. In no area was there a large field of either type, because, scattered in between them, were small hopgardens and orchards and small woodlands or copses.

THE FIRMIN FAMILY

The Bunce family, who had lived at Crowdleham for some two hundred years, left Kemsing at the beginning of the nineteenth century. The house and sixty-four acres, together with the Great Tithes which accrued from sales of corn, grain and hay, were sold by auction at the Royal Oak Hotel, Sevenoaks on 23rd July 1803, and were acquired in 1805 by Mr. Philip Douglas Firmin.

He was a button manufacturer and had a house and factory at No. 153, The Strand, London. In 1805 he employed a Mr. Smith, who was described as "a mason of Chart" by William Danks of Shoreham in his diary, to rebuild Crowdleham House.

Philip Firmin had two sons *(possibly four)* and two daughters. One of the latter, Eliza, died at the age of thirteen in 1819, and was buried in the chancel of Kemsing Church, where she is remembered by a wall tablet. The known sons were Philip Venner, and Robert Selby, and the second daughter was Ann. The Trustees appointed by Philip Firmin to administer his will were named as William Ongley and Samuel Marshall, and it is possible that they were also his sons, their surname of Firmin having been omitted in the document. Philip senior died on 6th January 1826, leaving £8,000 to his wife Mary and the use of the house for her life after which it would revert to the sons Philip and Robert. The business in The Strand was left to the sons but the house there was also left to his wife. She did not die until 1837, when she left the estate to Philip Venner Firmin, who leased the house and the land to Thomas Burgess the farmer. The latter was shown in the 1841 census as living there with his wife, his mother, his daughter, and some six servants. One of the Plum Tree Cottages was occupied by a shoemaker called Henry Russell and his wife Mary and seven children. The other cottage was empty.

Philip Venner Firmin sold the whole property to Mr. John Rogers, of Riverhill House, Sevenoaks in 1860.

1. The Revd. Maximilian Buck, BA
Vicar of Kemsing & Seal
1674/1720

2. The Revd. John Netherton Harwood, MA
Vicar of Kemsing & Seal
1838/1846

3. The Revd. Thomas Offspring Blackall, BA
Vicar of Kemsing & Seal
1846/1874

4. The Revd. George Bridges Lewis, MA
Vicar of Kemsing
1874/1888

5. The Revd. Thomas Carleton Skarratt, MA
Vicar of Kemsing
1889/1908

6. The Revd. Edward H. Stewart, MA
Vicar of Kemsing
1909/1924

7. The Revd. Ronald Victor Bristow, MA
Vicar of Kemsing
1924/1931

8. The Revd. Charles H.E. Freeman, MA
Vicar of Kemsing
1934/1936

9. The Revd. Vincent Macreth,
Vicar of Kemsing
1936/1939

10. The Revd. Albert Edward Scipiot, MA
Vicar of Kemsing
1939/1949

11. The Revd. John Aquila Lloyd, AKC
Vicar of Kemsing
1949/1956

12. The Revd. Geoffrey Maxwell Young, MA
Vicar of Kemsing & Priest-in-Charge of
Woodlands 1956/1967

13. The Revd. John Hermann Rahe Hughes, BA, Vicar of Kemsing & Woodlands 1967/1975

14. The Revd. Kenneth Percival Thomas Daniels, AKC, Vicar of Kemsing & Woodlands 1975/1983

15. The Revd. Richard William Bateman, AKC, Vicar of Kemsing & Woodlands 1983/1990

16. The Revd. Colin Clive Horn. C.Eng. Vicar of Kemsing & Woodlands 1991

Chapter 8
In Mr. Blackall's Time

Curates And Church Improvements

Much change was effected during the twenty-eight years of the vicariate of the Revd. Thomas Offspring Blackall, who was appointed vicar in 1846 after having served for three months as curate to the Revd. John Netherton Harward. Mr. Blackall realised that the combined parish of Kemsing and Seal was in need of sub-division. His work at Seal involved the extension and alteration of the church, where the west gallery was removed in 1855 and the north aisle erected. The first part of the parish to be hived off was Underriver, where St. Margaret's Church was opened as a Chapel of Ease in 1866. The following year, a new church on Seal Chart was dedicated to St. Lawrence. It had been built by the Wilkinson family of Seal Chart in memory of a young daughter, Mary Rachel, who died at St. Lawrence in the Isle of Wight. It was consecrated in June 1868.

On 6th August 1874, Kemsing and Seal parishes were separated by an Order in Council after having been united and served by the same rector or vicar for several hundred years.

As in previous incumbencies, during Mr. Blackall's time Kemsing was largely served by curates, of whom a whole string were appointed. As curates they usually lived in Seal, and some of them lodged with Stephen Groombridge who was the verger at Seal, living somewhere in Childsbridge Lane between Childsbridge Way and Meadowlands. This meant quite a walk for them, albeit across the fields, to Kemsing Church. The first of these young men, who were paid £80 per annum, was the Revd. F.O. Maine, and he was followed by the Revd. James Simpson in 1848; John Starkey in 1850; Charles Brook Bicknell in 1851; A. W. Gurney and Charles Wolf in 1852. In the same year, the Revd. G.B. Barker and the Revd. A. Boodle were appointed and in 1856 the Revd. L.J. Lovekin came with Mr. B.P. Thompson. 1857 saw the arrival of the Revd. J.M. Martin and 1860 the Revd. Vicesimus Knox Vade, who lodged at the Box House, Kemsing, with Mrs. Lillias Summers and her niece.

In 1862, the latest curate, the Revd. F. Philott was paid £100 per annum and the Revd. P. Ottey came in 1865 at the same figure, but he had to live in Seal, "there being no convenient residence procurable in the parish of Kemsing". The Revd. B.P. Thompson may have remained as a curate at Seal during all these changes, for in 1867, he was nominated by Mr. Horace Wilkinson to be the first incumbent of Seal St. Lawrence. Mr. Thompson was a son-in-law of Colonel Grevis James of Ightham Court, and a brother of Sir Matthew Thompson, 1st Baronet and Chairman of the Forth Bridge Committee and twice Mayor of Bedford. Kemsing's new curate in 1868 was the Revd. Morgan T. Pearson, who replaced Mr. Thompson but was given £120 per annum. He also had to live in Seal, some one and a half miles from Kemsing Church. There is some doubt as to the actual date of his appointment for, after having settled in, he wrote to the Archbishop of Canterbury on 29th March 1870 saying, "Dear Sir, I shall be much obliged if you would prevent the notification of my being licensed to this curacy as my appointment here has twice gone round the papers, and such advertisement I think more than sufficient".

In 1871 new curates were Messrs E.M. Banks and J. Chittenden. The Revd. E. Coupland who came in 1872 was paid at the reduced rate of £100 per annum. Mr. Blackall thus had some twenty-four curates working with him, but how much each had to do with Kemsing and Seal is not clear. Mr. Blackall himself lived at Godden Green, so it was probably necessary to have one curate living nearer the church at Seal while the other worked in Kemsing.

Apart from the restoration work done in Seal church and of the building of churches at Underriver and Seal St. Lawrence, Mr. Blackall saw to it that a certain amount of restoration work was carried out in Kemsing church. In 1870, the west gallery was removed and the oak box pews also. The latter were replaced by simple bench pews, leaving just one pair of the old benches at the west end of the nave. The sounding board of the pulpit was removed, and the floor of the chancel repaired. The 1870 restoration was paid for by a subscription fund amounting to £345. The building firm employed was Durtnells, who received £327, while the Architect, Mr. T. Graham Jackson was paid £18. The nave was restored, the roof retiled, weather-boarded and stripped, the walls were cleaned and coloured, and underfloor heating was installed. The interior of the roof was weather-boarded at this time, although a photo taken in 1869 shows that it had already been so boarded. The stone work of the west window was repaired in 1871 and new coloured glass put in by Mr. Blackall. This window had probably been plain since the destruction of the fourteenth and fifteenth century glass in 1826.

Further work undertaken in 1871 included repaving the nave with some old and some new tiles, making an open drain round the outside of the church and also a drain for the font, which was refixed. Repairs to the screen were made; a board floor installed under the belfry; and the west door re-hung. Still more work was carried out in 1873 when the chancel was re-ordered with seats in place of pews, and Minton tiles on the floor. Some stone steps were put under the screen leading up from the nave, and a new altar step and an iron communion rail put up. The Architects for this part of the work were Roper and Ogle, and the builder was Thomas Curtis.

The Vestry Book

All this repair work was organised by officials appointed at the Annual Meeting of the Vestry. This was held shortly after Easter each year and attended by any parishioners who were interested. Two churchwardens were appointed for the year together with overseers for the poor, guardians, waywardens, and constables. Whether these men kept minutes of their meetings before 1859 is not known, but in that year they provided a fine leather bound book in which Vestry Meeting minutes have been recorded every year for over a hundred and thirty years, the final entry being that for the year 1992. The early records tend to be lists of the appointments, but they also mention remarks made by the Archdeacon when he made his visit from time to time, usually later in the year. These remarks were in the form of recommendations for things that needed to be done to the fabric of the church together with advice to the people of the parish to conserve their heritage and not to destroy things of historic and cultural value.

Sometimes informative remarks were added to the formal reports, and these tell us something of the men who were responsible for the running of the parish church and village at that time.

Mid-Nineteenth Century Families And Developments

By the middle of the 19th century the most numerous family in the village were the Kipps. First recorded in 1561, when a child was baptised, this family numbered twenty-two in 1851, living in five households. They were rivalled by the Holden family, and the related Whitlocks, twenty-three people living in four houses. The Bowyers occupied five different houses and accounted for seventeen people, while the Skinners and the Reeves and the Dykes numbered fourteen, thirteen and seven people respectively. These families were all to inter-marry as the century progressed, and there are several descendants of them still living here.

The Holden group were descended from James Holden, a blacksmith who had plied his trade in several villages before settling in Kemsing at some time before 1813 when Hezro, the first of his children to be born in Kemsing, was baptised. He had eight children, who all shared the initials H.H. as they were baptised Harriet, Hezekiah, Henrietta, Hezro, Heli, Hariph, Hetebath and Helen. The two older brothers were also blacksmiths, and when they were able to take over the business, James became a beer seller. He used one of the rooms in his cottage, which was one of five that stood in the High Street where the Old Forge and New Cottages are now, as a public room, the precursor of the public house. Hezekiah and Hezro lived opposite in the present Vicarage.

The eldest son, Hezekiah, married Sally Bowyer and they had seven children. After her death he married again, Mary Wickenden, and in 1850, they emigrated to Australia with one daughter, leaving behind three of the older boys to be looked after by Hezro and his wife Jane (nee Bowyer and sister to Sally), and two more in Sevenoaks Union House.

One of the boys followed them to Australia later on. Hezro, having five children of his own, needed a larger house, and in about 1868 he built Clement House in the High Street. It was probably on the foundations of an earlier house, because the present cellar seems to be much older than the house above it. The eldest daughter, Harriet, also emigrated but this time to New Zealand, while the second daughter, Henrietta, stayed in this country and married George Whitlock. The Whitlocks eventually came to live in Dynes Farm, with their fourteen children. The brothers-in-law, Hezro Holden and George Whitlock both served as churchwardens. Hezro was also one of the first people in Kemsing to handle the post, being made receiver of letters in 1870, a post he relinquished in 1872 when his nephew, Andrew, was appointed Kemsing's first postmaster, a position he held until he died aged 90 in 1929.

One of the younger daughters, Helen, married Edmund James Cope, the schoolmaster, in 1852 but unfortunately she died in 1853. The matriarch of the family, Sarah Holden, survived her husband

James by many years, living on in one of the row of cottages which she owned in the High Street. In the 1851 census she was described as a "Proprietor of Houses" yet she was content to leave two of her grandsons in the Union House.

The Bowyers, Richard and Sarah, arrived in Kemsing about 1790 when their son Richard was baptised. Two of their daughters married Holdens, Sarah to Hezekiah and Jane to Hezro, while one of their grandsons, George Bowyer, married Mary Ann Holden, a grand-daughter of James Holden. Some of the Bowyers were thatchers.

The Kipps family had probably lived in the village well before the 16th century. They went on to populate the parish well into the 20th century, many of them serving as useful citizens and taking on such responsible posts as churchwarden and parish clerk.

The Reeves were for the most part agricultural labourers, although some later became blacksmiths. They married into the Dykes and Kipps families.

The Skinners and Dykes were also mostly agricultural labourers. The term Agricultural Labourer *(shortened to Ag. Lab)* is one that was used by the census enumerators to describe any man who worked on the land. Women, and children too, worked on the farms at certain times of the year, but they were never called Ag.Labs. The agricultural labourer was often a very skilled worker, and the occupations covered by this term include shepherds, cow men, hedgers, ditchers, ploughmen and their team mates, waggoners, grooms, and woodreeves or woodmen.

Not much is known about the public houses in Kemsing prior to the middle of the nineteenth century, when directories giving particulars of the people living in the various parishes of Kent were published. These *(including Bagshaw's in 1847 and Melville's and Kelly's later)* gave some details of the publicans. The Bell Inn, probably the oldest in the parish, was run by Mr. William Jeffrey, and The Chequers at Heverham by Mrs Sarah Bennett. Adam Bloxall followed Mrs Bennett and was himself succeeded there in 1870 by Edwin Meades and by John Woodman in 1874.

The Wheatsheaf is not mentioned until 1858 when William

Geering is shown as a beer seller rather than as a publican, but in 1866 the name "The Wheatsheaf" appears as that of a recognised public house.

Not many people in Kemsing had the right to vote for Members of Parliament, but in 1874 the list of twenty-four included not only the gentry like the Revd. Edmund Boscawen Evelyn and William John Evelyn of St. Clere, but also some publicans, farmers and leading tradesmen.

The opening of new railway stations at this time linked Otford with Sevenoaks and later with Maidstone, and thus brought Kemsing into closer touch with London. This encouraged new residents who were prepared to travel to and from the City. The Bat and Ball Station at Sevenoaks was opened in 1868, and Kemsing Station on 1st June, 1874. There was an exchange platform between Otford and Bat and Ball, to link Sevenoaks with Maidstone. The first station master at Kemsing was Edwin James Willis *(1875-1877)* and his successors included Barnaby Barber *(1879-1900)*, William Nash *(1900)*, William Henry Pettman *(1903-1917)*, William Knight *(1919)*, Walter Edwin Tapsell *(1921)*, and Thomas Christopher Foster.

An amateur survey of the wild flowers around the Noah's Ark railway bridge in the 1960s revealed that the soil that composed the ramps up to the bridge was mostly chalk, whereas the surrounding fields were of clay. The conclusion formed was that the material for these ramps had been brought down the line when the railway was being constructed, and came from the cuttings through the chalk hills between Otford and Swanley.

It has been suggested that some of the houses in Noah's Ark were built especially for men who worked on the laying of the railway lines. This is not born out by the information given in the census returns for 1881 and 1891. In 1881 there were two platelayers and one railway porter living as lodgers in Noah's Ark, while six other men worked for the railway but did not live in Noah's Ark. In 1891 four platelayers lived there, and one porter and one signalman lived with the station master in the station house.

SEPARATE PARISHES OF KEMSING AND SEAL

The hiving off of some of his huge parish was part of a scheme that Mr. Blackall had formulated under which Seal and Underriver would become separate parishes with their own incumbents. This scheme was not mentioned in his will, written in 1871, nor in the notes of the Archdeacon's Visitations of 1872, but by 1874 it was known to the patron of the living, Mr. Mortimer Sackville-West of Knole, and to Mr. R. Few, father of the curate at Seal. Both these gentlemen wrote to Archbishop Campbell Tait of Canterbury, supporting a suggestion made to them by Mr. Blackall, that the living should be sold by Mr. Sackville-West to Mr. R. Few for a sum of £3,000.

Mr. Few wrote on 17th April giving the addresses of Mr. Sackville-West; Mr. Turner, a former churchwarden of Seal now living at Lee; and Mr. Miller of Greenwich Vicarage, and desiring the Archbishop's opinion on two points raised by Mr. Sackville-West, viz "as to the propriety of his selling the next turn to me for £3,000, appropriating at least £2,000 for the improvement of Kempsing (sic) and Underriver, and as to the suitability of my own son for such a post in which your Grace so kindly promised to make enquiries". The last remark indicates that Mr. Few had already raised the question about his son with the Archbishop.

Mr. Sackville-West, who was to become the first Baron Sackville in 1888, wrote on 20th April 1874 "upon the following subject which has been brought to my notice by Mr. Blackall, the Vicar of Seal *(sic)*, of which living I am Patron. The following is Mr. Blackall's proposal: That it would be to the advantage of the souls upon the charge, that it should be divided into three separate benefices. To carry out this proposal it would be necessary to sell the next presentation *(upon Mr. Blackall's resigning)* and that the proceeds which would amount to £3,000 should be appropriated by me to building a Vicarage House at Kemsing and another at Underriver, say £1,000 each, the remaining £1,000 as an extra endowment for Kemsing".

He goes on to say that Mr. Blackall had made enquiries and

found that Mr. R. Few, a well-known solicitor and active supporter of the Church in London, would pay £3,000 for the living. Mr. Sackville-West sought the Archbishop's opinion of the whole arrangement and of Mr. Few himself, adding that "owing to the number and variety of inhabitants it is necessary that the Vicar of Seal should be a man with tact and discretion as well as a thorough gentleman of sound church principles. By this I mean NOT very high church, as I myself do not approve of Ritualism".

The Archbishop lost no time in replying, for his memorandum on the subject is dated 23rd April. It indicated that His Grace gave general approval for the scheme as he felt that it was highly desirable that vicarage houses should be built at Kemsing and Underriver and resident incumbents appointed. He would like more particulars, however, on some points, viz:

1. What would be the income of each benefice when the division had taken place. A donation of £1,000 each could be met in each case by a grant of a similar sum from the Ecclesiastical Commissioners providing that more pressing cases did not exhaust the funds at their disposal for such purposes, and he noted that at present prices a parsonage house could not be built under £1,600 at the lowest estimate.

2. It was important for him to know the extent and population of each of the three parishes, which information Mr. Blackall would no doubt be able to supply.

The memorandum went on to note that Mr. Few senior was well-known to the Archbishop as an earnest supporter of all good works in the church, and that the Bishop of Rochester gave a high character to the Revd. C.E. Few who was proposed as the new incumbent of Seal Vicarage.

The Revd. Mr. Miller and Mr. Turner also lost no time in replying, the former commenting that Mr. Charles Few was a thorough gentleman, had a nice wife, was High Church but not ritualistic. The latter said he had been churchwarden at Seal when Mr. Few was curate there and that Mr. Few was liked by all in the parish, rich and poor, and that he preached plain, simple sermons, short and to the point. Mr. Blackall was asked to read the memorandum from the Archbishop and to provide the answers to the questions raised. This he did, adding that he would be in London the next week and would be prepared to "attend at Lambeth upon receiving an intimation of the hour at 39, Queen's Gate". he also added a P.S. "It would seem that Mr. Few desires a speedy settlement of the matter as far as he is concerned".

The information supplied by Mr. Blackall was that the gross income from the tithe rent charges of Kemsing in 1872/3 was £151.12s.0d. There was a small tenement with a garden called The Old Vicarage which was let at £6 per annum. He hoped to exchange this with one of the chief proprietors of the parish for a piece of ground suitable for the erection of a parsonage house. *(The Old Vicarage stood on the site of the four houses in St. Edith Road called Vicarage Cottages, and the other piece of ground was all that land now occupied by the Youth Hostel, Queensmead, Cleves Cottage, Teron, the new burial ground and the church hall and field).*

Mr. Blackall went on to say that he hoped that the Commissioners would add a substantial sum to the £1,000 for Kemsing, but that he had found that clergymen of private means were often willing to accept an independent position of which the income was small, provided that there was or was to be a comfortable residence and that the parochial circumstances were favourable. The population of Kemsing at the last census *(1871)* was four-hundred and eight, and the area of the parish was 2,388 acres. Mr. Blackall sent this missive on 28th April, the day after Mr. Sackville-West had also written to the Archbishop, including an invitation to His Grace to "consider Knole as your HQs when next you are coming to this part of Kent". So the whole correspondence occupied no more than eleven days.

On the 11th August 1874 the London Gazette published a notice and details of an Order in Council dated 6th August at the Court of Osborne House, Isle of Wight, the Queen's Most Excellent Majesty being present. The Order sets out the whole situation and proposals in detail, and even adds the odd *(to to-day's way of thinking)* statement that "the inhabitants of Seal shall be exclusively entitled to accommodation in the chapel of that proposed parish and they shall not be entitled to any accommodation in the parish church of Kemsing". The Queen was, with the advice of her Council, pleased to order that the scheme of the Lord Archbishop of Canterbury be carried into effect, but a few more months were to pass before it was so effected. On 25th September Mr. Blackall wrote to Lambeth again, trying to hurry up the appointment of Mr. Few to Seal, because the churchwardens "have to provide services in the two churches on the Sunday following my resignation on the first of October". He had already had to volunteer to take services at Kemsing because the Revd. George Bridges Lewis could not be presented to that living in time. In fact that gentleman was writing on the same day to a Mr. Lee, at the Archbishop's office in Broad Sanctuary, to say that Mr. Sackville-West was to present him to the living, but that the date of the presentation could not be before 19th October as he could not leave Northaw Parsonage in Northamptonshire until then. In the long run Mr. Blackall did resign on the first of October and Mr. Few was instituted to Seal on the second while Mr. Lewis was instituted to Kemsing on the third of November. Even then the scheme was not entirely implemented for a while as Mr. Few appeared to misunderstand the conditions of the settlement and argued for a while that Underriver should not be separated from Seal. Mr. Mortimer Sackville-West had to intervene in that matter and also in the matter of the building of the vicarage at Kemsing, which was held up for some time because of a delay in the negotiations for the exchange of land.

KEMSING
KENT
CANTERBURY
PILGRIMS WAY

Chapter 9
Kemsing On Its Own

A Victorian Parson

The arrival of the Revd. George Bridges Lewis as the first Vicar of Kemsing alone marked the beginning of a new phase in the life of the people of Kemsing, and a first step towards a more dignified and enlightened lifestyle for many. Mr. Lewis was typical of the Victorian, caring priest, who was ready to help his parishioners in every way, but was not slow to express his condemnation of any form of misbehaviour. He came here from Northamptonshire alone, because there was no house suitable for a family home. At first he tried the Old Parsonage House in St. Edith's Road, but found it quite useless as a vicarage, so he lodged for a while at Crowdleham. A map prepared at this time marks Crowdleham as the Vicarage, and gives the church dedication as St. Edith's.

Meanwhile, Mr. Mortimer Sackville-West, as Lord of the Manor, was providing a vicarage. To do so, the Parsonage House and the glebeland behind it were sold, and a plot of land off the Pilgrims Way purchased, on which a house was built in 1875/1876 at a cost of about £2,000. The vicar's wife and family then arrived, with some of their servants, including a gardener, Mr. Haines, who was given Wallis House, now the Vicarage, as his home. Mr. Lewis found the men of the village very rough and ready. He blamed the publicans for allowing heavy drinking on Saturday nights, which often led to rowdiness and fighting in the street. Men would go up to the Rising Sun at weekends, and on returning down the hill would drink again at The Bell and The Wheatsheaf, a practice which the vicar strove to eliminate.

Finding that the residents of Noah's Ark had to come up to St. Edith's well for water, he had a separate well sunk in the forecourt of a mission hut which was built in 1887 where the Kemsing Coach-works stand now.

THE NEW SCHOOL

Education for Kemsing children had been minimal up to 1847. In that year a National School was built in Main Street *(now Nos. 17 and 19 St. Edith Road)*, and Mr. E. J. Cope was appointed master. Miss Rigby followed him until 1879, when she was succeeded by Miss Caroline Hall and Miss Mary Kipps. The latter was a pupil teacher. There was also a paid monitor called Sophia Ligney. Miss Hall retired in 1885 and she received a parting present of a travelling bag, a carriage clock, and books of poems by Tennyson and Longfellow.

Feeling that the education of the children at this school was not good enough, Mr. Lewis was instrumental in raising a fund for the purpose of erecting a new and better appointed school.

The plans for this building with a house for the headmaster were scrutinised by him, and just before building began, he caused everything to be reversed, so that the house was at the west end of the schoolroom rather than, as planned by the architects, at the east end. The builders must have enjoyed this reversal! The school moved into the new building in 1885.

Among the contributors to the school fund were Mr. Mark W. Collet, Mr. Barclay Field, Mr. John Rogers, Lord Amherst, Sir Charles Mills, Bt., Mr H. Bingham-Mildmay, Mr. Alexander, Mr. Rudgard, Mr.Stonham, Mr. Bridge, and the Revd. G.B. Lewis.

These people, with fifteen others, raised £1,179. The architects were Messrs. Ford and Hesketh, and the builders were Messrs. Wiltshire & Sons, of Sevenoaks.

The new headmaster, Mr. Albert Bennett, employed his daughter as a sewing teacher, but he was in the post for only a few months, being succeeded by Mr. Albert George Jordan, assisted by his wife Jane, and Miss Mary Kipps. The new school started well by abolishing slates and pencils and using pens and ink. This was the beginning of a long reign of thirty-six years by Mr. Jordan. The headmasters who followed him were Mr. Leonard L. Lowing *(1924-1950)*; Mr. Stanley R. Smart *(1951-1969)*; Mr. Allan Gilbert *(1969-1985)*; and Mr. Paul Hillman *(1985-)*. The old school building in St. Edith Road was used as a boys club in the 1890s, while the 1885 school, apart from the house, was leased to the Parish Council in 1992 for use as an extra venue for parish activities. Another small benefaction by Mr Lewis took the form of installing a lamp on a pole at the entrance to the path leading to the Post Office in the old cottages that stood in the High Street, where the Old Forge is now.

In 1878 a small vestry was built on the north side of the chancel incorporating an old window frame that had been in the north wall of the chancel and is, in fact, still in use in the present day choir vestry.

The new Vicar's daughters took a great interest in their father's work in the parish, and in 1877 they provided half the cost of a small organ which was installed the next year in the arch that linked the chancel with the new vestry. They also gave a silver flagon to mark a confirmation at Kemsing by Dr. Parry, Bishop of Dover.

In 1880, Mr. Lewis paid for the design and fixing of a stained glass window in the east end of the church. The work was carried out by the firm of Dixon and Vesey, and the design was in three lights, showing Christ on the Cross, flanked by St. Mary and St. John. *(This window, much admired by John Newman in "Pevsner's Buildings of Kent", was moved in 1902 to its present site in the south wall of the chancel)*.

At the same time, the 14th or 15th century St. Anne window in the sanctuary was repaired.

In 1881 Mrs. Margaret Smith of Heverham repaired the large window in the south wall of the nave in memory of her brother George.. It was designed and executed by Dixons and it is said to have held plain quarries with a border of foliage.

Mr. Lewis provided a handsome brass bucket for carrying water to the font for christenings. It is still used. He also gave a brass book rest for the altar, and to improve the lighting of the church he bought six hanging oil lamps and negotiated the purchase of a large brass candelabra which had hung in the church of St. Giles, Shipbourne, until 1881 when that church was rebuilt by the Cazalet family. In 1892, after their departure from Kemsing, Mr. Lewis's family gave to Kemsing church as a memorial to his son, Frank, a brass lectern. This was eventually replaced in 1914, by an oak lectern, which has in turn been replaced by a small, plain wooden one. The oak lectern was a gift from the Revd. E.H. Stewart in memory of his mother who died in 1908. It was designed by J. Ninian Comper, and as such is an item of national interest and value and deserves to be preserved.

An interesting insight into the working of the Vestry is given by the report that in 1878 Mr. Dawson, who lived at Stonepitts, was proposed as the new waywarden by the Revd. Edmund Boscawen Evelyn, owner of St. Clere. Mr. George Turner of Heverham was also nominated, and he received nine votes against Mr. Dawson's eight. Mr. Evelyn then demanded a poll, so the meeting was adjourned to the following week when Mr. Turner was elected.

At The Bell, William Jeffrey left in 1874 and George Mills took over. At The Chequers were Henry Briggs and John Woodman from 1874 to 1881, when Mrs. Sarah Woodman was the licensee until 1895. The Wheatsheaf was still regarded as a beer house until it was rebuilt in 1880, when the Geering family were the publicans.

THE ARCHDEACON'S VIEWS

An Archdeacon's Visitation Report for 1880 gives interesting insights into the lives of the villagers and reflects on the moral and spiritual conditions obtaining in late Victorian days. He said the population were mostly labouring poor, and of a regular congregation of a hundred and fifty only twenty were regular communicants and ten occasional. This low figure he put down to the presence of "dissenters among the professing Christians", and to the fact that seats, although not let for money, were "appropriated by the various classes" and were allocated by the churchwardens according to their ideas of what was suitable and the habits of the various families.

The Chapel in St. Edith's Road was said to have started as a Methodist Chapel but had become Bible Christian. *(In the 1950s this chapel was used as a meeting place by villagers and then converted into a piano repair shop and a bungalow)*. There was one Baptist family in the village but no Roman Catholics were recorded. The publicans came in for criticism for not regulating the amount drunk by their customers, and one of the churchwardens was reprimanded for not being regular in his duties. The Archdeacon recorded that both poor people and rich were "strangely indifferent to what takes place at a grave after the service is over", but he did not explain what he meant by this criticism. He mentioned a parochial library although no details were given as to how many books were held or where they were housed. Very few people were on poor relief, but the moral condition was very low. The people were rough, headstrong, coarse and not selfcontrolled. And finally it was even recommended that "notably immoral people" should not receive burial service at the hands of the clergy.

Property changed hands from time to time and the main landowners in 1878 were Earl Amherst, Mr. Richard R. Behrens, Mr. John Thornton Rogers, and Mr. George Turner. In 1881, there was a sale of five lots, which included Castle Bank, 1 and 3 St. Edith's Road, 35 to 53 West End, Well Cottage, Rose Cottage and a block of land east of The Landway.

The census return for that year *(1881)* revealed that the population was now four hundred and forty three, living in eighty-three houses, indicating that just one house had been built in the previous ten years.

Yew Tree Cottages in the High Street were built in 1884 by Wiltshires of Sevenoaks. One of the men working on this contract was Mr. Thomas Skinner, whose three daughters continued to live in one of the cottages well into the 20th century.

Water was still only available in wells. Most of these have since been filled in, but they were to be found behind the cottages in the High Street,the south side of West End, St. Edith's Road, and even on Castle Bank. A pump is still to be seen outside No. 1 Park Lane Villas, which was not built until 1909. Other cottagers had to carry drinking water from St. Edith's well, while using water from rainwater butts, streams or ponds for other purposes. Perhaps the unluckiest families in this respect were those living in the cottage called Cold Banks, which stood by a shallow pond on the top of Side Hill, just below the cross that was later erected there. Yet when in 1886 thirteen inhabitants met to consider the possibility of supplies of water being brought to Kemsing by the Sevenoaks Water Company, the suggestion was turned down, although Mr. Barclay Field and Mr. Thomas Stonham, the Churchwarden, and one other were in favour. A second meeting of fifteen people held the following week agreed that no action should be taken, thus condemning the people of Kemsing to dependence on well water and rain water for another quarter century or more.

The Vicarage in 1876

The station masters from the opening of the Station in 1874 to 1900 were Edwin James Willis and Barnaby Barber. Mr. Willis became the butler at St. Clere, and was evidently on duty there at the time of the 1881 census for his wife Harriet and their four children are shown as living in Heverham without him. Barnaby's nineteen year old son, Arthur, served as the goods clerk at the station.

Queen Victoria's Jubilee in 1887 was marked by the granting of a holiday to the school children.

Farewell To A Well-Loved Vicar

When Mr. Bridges Lewis announced that he was moving to another parish *(Frinstead near Sittingbourne)* his parishioners decided to make a presentation to him on his departure. The subscription fund was collected by Mr. Thomas Stonham of Dynes Farm who was churchwarden. The sum amounted to £61 and was completely subscribed by residents of Kemsing.

In July 1888 "a goodly gathering of the parishioners of Kemsing" in the school included the Vicar and his two daughters *(Mrs. Lewis was unfortunately not well)*, Sir Mark W. Collet and Lady Collet, Mr & Mrs Thomas Stonham, the Headmaster, Mr. Jordan, and many others. Sir Mark opened the proceedings by reminding those present of the immense impression Mr. Lewis had made on the parish during his fourteen years as Vicar. When appointed to be the first Vicar of Kemsing alone, after the division from Seal, he had found the parish to be in a poor state in many ways.

At the end of his ministry, a new vicarage and school had been built, and many other improvements made in the village. Sir Mark went on to thank the Vicar and concluded by tendering to him and his family the best wishes of the people of Kemsing for their future happiness.

The actual presentation of gifts was made by Mr. Stonham who handed to Mr. Lewis "a very handsome silver breakfast dish" on which was inscribed "Presented to the Reverend George Bridges Lewis MA by his parishioners and neighbours on his leaving

Kemsing, in affectionate remembrance of his ministry amongst them for fourteen years. July 1888". To Miss Ann Madeline Lewis and Miss Frances Louisa Lewis he presented a pair of handsome gold bracelets, on which were engraved the names of the recipients and "In affectionate remembrance from Kemsing July 1888".

In his reply Mr. Lewis thanked the people of Kemsing for their help with special mention of Sir Mark, and he thought that the "erection of the school room was a matter for much thankfulness". The gifts were accompanied by an address which contained the signatures of about one hundred and sixty parishioners. It was beautifully presented, and read "Kemsing July 1888 to the Reverend George Bridges Lewis MA, we the parishioners of Kemsing by your acceptance of the accompanying silver dish, with gold bracelets for each of your daughters, as a mark of our esteem and a slight recognition of the great good, both spiritual and material effected by you during your residence of fourteen years in this parish, do desire to express our deep regret at the departure from among us of you and your family and our sincere hopes for your and their future welfare".

LEADING FAMILIES

Among the families who were in Kemsing in the last half of the 19th century were the Rudgards of Crowdleham. William Rudgard was of independent means and he came from Lincoln with his wife, son and daughter. They employed a staff of five in 1871 but only two in 1881. Not one of these people was Kemsing born, but Mr. Rudgard took an active interest in the village and was churchwarden from 1870 to 1875. He presented to the church the two sanctuary chairs and the brass offertory plate which are still in use.

The farmland at Crowdleham was worked by the Browning family. William Browning came to Kemsing from East Malling with his wife and sons, George and William, and daughter Elizabeth about the year 1844. Their farmhouse, now called Crowdleham

Lodge, was next to Crowdleham House.

William's brother Alfred also came and acted as his partner in the farm, which comprised some two hundred acres, employing seven agricultural labourers. By 1871 the acreage had diminished to one hundred and twenty, employing only five labourers and two boys. William's elder son, George, took over the farm when his father died, and William, the younger son, was also a farmer. The latter went into partnership with Henry Wellband of Otford, who had entered into the steam-threshing business, travelling round from farm to farm throughout the county. George helped to finance this venture but unfortunately it was not immediately successful and George was obliged to surrender his farm. He and his family went to live at The Bell Inn, where his father-in-law, William Jeffrey was the publican. He became what the census return of 1871 called "a steam threshing machine driver out of work". It is said that he never recovered from the loss of his farm, and that he met a sad death. However, one of his sons, Ernest Charles Browning, years later did, by dint of hard work, redeem his father's name and reputation by becoming a successful farmer, but that story belongs to Otford, where the family still live. After the Brownings had left, the farmhouse at Crowdleham was empty for a while.

Old Wybournes was the house for a few years of Randolph Caldecott, the illustrator of children's books. With his wife and his sister, Mrs. Brind, he employed a coachman, a cook, and a chambermaid, none of whom was born in Kemsing. Many of the letters he wrote while living in Kemsing were illustrated by sketches of views and people of Kemsing.

At Heverham, Manor House Farm was occupied in 1851 by Mrs. Elizabeth Turner, who employed twelve labourers to run two hundred and fifty acres, while her son farmed a further two hundred acres with eight labourers. In the house they employed four servants. Ten years later, they were working three hundred acres together, with just nine labourers and one servant. In 1871 Mrs. Turner had died, and George was farming six hundred and fifty acres with sixteen labourers and seven boys and one servant.

His sister, Mrs. Margaret Smith, a widow, lived with him and after his death in 1880 she remained the occupier of the farmhouse and employed a shepherd, ten labourers and six boys on the farm.

She was the founder of a charity in Kemsing by which a small sum of money was expended year by year for supplying coal to needy and elderly people at the discretion of the vicar. As the income from a capital sum of £212 brought a yearly income of less than £25, the Charity Commissioners ruled in 1992 that the charity and its aims must be absorbed by the church.

St. Edith's Farm, owned by William Guest, was occupied by Sarah, the widow of Amos Swaisland and her son James in 1841, and they were succeeded in 1851 by John Hyde who had three hundred and twenty-two acres and employed sixteen men. Several changes were made in the next few years during which the farmers were Joseph Larking and later his son, Jabez, and later still George Cawston, who farmed four hundred and twenty-four acres with fourteen men, four boys and seven women.

George Whitlock, who has been mentioned before in connection with the Holden family, worked Dynes Farm for some fifteen years and while there raised a family of fourteen children. He was for some years churchwarden and took great interest in the affairs of the village. He was succeeded in 1857 by Thomas Stonham who was also a great pillar of strength in the parish acting as churchwarden for no less than twenty-eight years, and the family continued to serve the parish in this way when his son, Harry, became churchwarden.

There were several smaller farms, in fact as small as eight acres and they were run by such people as Henry Bowyer, William Geering, Edwin Meades, William Wigsell, James Upton, Suzanne and John Goose, and James Stewart.

Mr. Barclay Field held a great deal of land in Heverham and in 1875 he bought several hundred acres of Dynes Farm, north and south of the Pilgrims Way, from Earl Amherst. He paid £2,170 plus a further £750 for two smaller plots. On the area north of the Pilgrims Way, between Row Dow and Chalky Lane, he had a house built and pleasure gardens laid out and planted with many specimen trees. He called the house Beechy Lees and made it his second home, his main home being in London. He resided in Beechy Lees *(now St Michael's School)* long enough to participate in Kemsing parish affairs, and was Overseer of the poor in 1884. He contributed about one quarter of the amount needed to build the new school in 1885, and £1,191 of the £3,436 needed to build the north aisle of the church in 1890. He died on 7th November 1892, and his brother George and his sister, Mrs. Marsham, had the chancel screen in the church restored and completed with a rood loft in his memory. This work was carried out by the woodcarver, William Unsworth.

The brother, Mr. George Hanbury Field, who lived at Ashurst Park, Tunbridge Wells, inherited Beechy Lees, which indicates that Mr. Barclay Field had no children. George evidently also used the house as a second home, because he became people's churchwarden in 1899, shortly before dying on 24th July 1900. He and his wife, Emily Maude, had two sons. Reginald George was born on 16th August 1895 and baptised in Kemsing Church on 12th October that year. The other son, Cuthbert Arthur Morris, inherited Beechy Lees and he died at Ashurst Park on 3rd November 1917. It seems that the house was sometimes completely unoccupied because in 1881 the census return contains no reference to it, not even to a caretaker.

When Mr. Barclay Field became the landowner at Heverham in place of Archdeacon Berens in the 1880s, he restored some of the houses, marking them on the gables with his initials, BF. He employed bailiffs to look after the farms, and they lived in Walnut Tree Cottage. They were in 1887 Daniel Underhill and in 1890 Richard Smerdon. The estate carpenters included Allan Botting, who was a regular member of the church choir and one of Kemsing's first parish councillors. Unfortunately he died suddenly of typhoid when only thirty-six years old. His funeral, held in August 1896, was long remembered in the village for the vast number of people who attended and for the fact that they were all dispersed suddenly from the graveside by a violent thunderstorm. The Vicar of that time, Mr. Skarratt, erected the ornamental covered gate at the west end of the churchyard in his memory. It was built, and the woodcarving done by Messrs. Riches and Whitehead at St. Clere. Mr. Riches, who was one of the estate carpenters from 1897 to 1926, was churchwarden from 1915 to 1926, and also Chairman of the Parish Council from 1905-06.

There was sometimes a steward looking after Beechy Lees House and in 1895 this was John Busridge. As Mr. Cuthbert Field did not reside in the house, it was let to Mr. James Murray Tulloch JP, from 1915 until it ceased to be the property of the Field family.

The Field family were engaged in the business of brewing beer, and the names Barclay, Hanbury and Field, have occurred in the names of several brewing companies. Barclay Field was said to be responsible for building the first oasthouses in the Kemsing and Otford district, but if so it was before he came to live in the parish, which was not until 1875.

The Botting Gate

Chapter 10
The End Of The Victorian Era

The Families Of Skarratt, Collet And Bridge

The Revd. G.B. Lewis was succeeded as Vicar by the Revd. the Hon. E.V.R. Powis, a son of Lord Lilford. He was a widower with two sons aged twenty-two and eighteen, but it is not known whether they came to Kemsing with him. He seems to have made little or no impression in the village during his short term as vicar. In fact, the record of services taken in that time bears an entry which marked the last service which he took in Kemsing church and against it in an unknown hand are the words "laus deo". This indicates the feeling that at least one member of his congregation must have had for him.

He was succeeded by the Revd. Thomas Carleton Skarratt. The Skarratts with the Collets and Bridges were the leading families in Kemsing for some twenty years. The Skarratts were at the Vicarage *(now the Youth Hostel)*, the Collets at St. Clere, and the Bridges at the "Old" Wybournes.

Beginning with the Skarratts, their connection with the village centres on the Revd. T.C. Skarratt, who was vicar from 1889 to 1908. He was a bachelor but entertained extensively at the vicarage, his guests being members of his large family and his many friends. These included his mother and father, his brother, Sydney and his five sisters. To accommodate these guests he had the vicarage extended by filling in the angle formed at the east end by the original building. This part, which is easily distinguished by the red brick used, contrasting with the earlier stonework, included a small private chapel.

The earliest known Skarratt was one Richard, a bell founder of Cheshire, who was born about 1770. His son, Robert, married a girl called Sarah, whose surname was possibly Carleton, because their son was christened Carleton, a name that was to persist throughout the family from then onwards. Robert and Sarah came to London, where their six children were born at Cripplegate. Young Carleton was apprenticed to a clock maker as were others of the family. At least three of them moved to the west country on qualifying as clock makers, John and Thomas to Worcester, and Carleton to Kington in Herefordshire. The Kington branch grew rapidly, as Carleton's son Thomas raised a family of ten children. One of these, Charles, was not content to remain in Kington all his life, and he decided to emigrate to Australia with a neighbour, Walter Hall, who later became his brother-in-law. They settled in the neighbourhood of Geelong where there was a rapid growth in the population because of the discovery of gold. Charles opened a hostel for the miners, many of whom had come from Cornwall, where the tin and copper industries had recently failed. Walter Hall started a store supplying the miners and what families they had with them, with day to day necessities.

In Geelong, Charles Carleton Skarratt married Mary Ellen Wren, a girl who had come out from London. They had five children between 1855 and 1862 and then moved to Melbourne where four more were born. Finally they moved north to Sydney where Charles Sydney and his twin sisters, Daisy Wren and Violet Hall were born. Eight of these children came to know Kemsing, for in 1881, Charles and Mary Ellen brought them all back to England, Charles having become very rich through his connection with Walter Hall, and the Mount Morgan Mining Company. It is a somewhat shady story, with the Halls as the villains of the piece, and Charles Skarratt as a comparatively innocent participator. After some time in Sydney, where they had set up home in the district now known as Kings Cross, they moved up to Rockhampton where new goldfields had been opened up. There Charles opened a new hotel. Nearby, two brothers called Morgan were living on a small mountain, trying to eke out a living by farming, when it was found that the mountain was virtually made of gold. A company was founded to work the gold, and Walter Hall was one of the first shareholders. He rather cunningly edged the Morgan brothers out of the firm by astutely buying up shares whenever there was a share issue and finally became the chief shareholder. He invited Charles to buy a large block of shares for something like £6,000, and it was this investment and the profits made at the hotel that enabled Charles to move back to Sydney where he built himself a large house at Summer Hill, called - what else - "Carleton". It remains there today, and is used as a children's home.

On arriving in England again, the family took up residence in London. The eldest son, Thomas Carleton, who was always called just Carleton in the family, had preceded the rest of the family and had gone up to Cambridge after visiting his namesake uncle in Kington. The latter always referred to this nephew in his diary as "Australian Tom". The daughters were sent to finishing schools in England and Paris, whilst Sydney went to Monkton Combe School in Somerset.

Thomas Carleton graduated in 1884, and was ordained in 1885. After being a curate at Christchurch, Paddington, he became Vicar of Kemsing in 1889, being presented to the living by Lord Sackville, the Lord of the Manor.

As time went on, all the daughters married. Emily's husband was Arthur F. McQuade, whose grandson the Revd. Fred McQuade, visited Kemsing from Canada in 1988. Amy was twice married, firstly to T.H. Keigwin, and then to Roland Pope. Lucy Ann married Charles Theobald.

The eldest sister, Mary Ellen, was first married to Mr. John Gardyne and after his death she married Mr. John Edward Charles Bridge of Old Wybournes, Kemsing. He was Chief Official of the Post Office and his first wife, Edith Mary, had died in 1888. Another wedding took place on the 3rd June 1903 in Kemsing Church between the Vicar's youngest sister, Violet, and Mr. John Sargent Bridge, stepson of her elder sister, Mary Ellen. Daisy and Lucy Ann were bridesmaids, and the service was conducted by the Bishop of Kensington assisted by the Revd. Thomas Carleton Skarratt, brother of the bride.

The families of Bridge and Skarratt may have been known to each other before Carleton became Vicar of Kemsing. In Admiralty House, Kirribilli, Sydney, Australia, is a window holding a representation of the coat of arms of Admiral Cyprian Bridge. While on duty there, the Admiral was more than likely to have been a visitor to the Skarratts' house at Summer Hill. Cyprian was the eldest of the three brothers of John E.C. Bridge, the others being Major General Thomas Field Duncombe, and Brigadier General Sir Charles Henry. The Bridge coat of arms can be seen in the chancel of Kemsing Church. In the first and fourth quarters there is a representation of a bridge, as a heraldic pun on the name.

The presence in the parish of these families over a period of some twenty years, and of others like the Fields of Beechy Lees, must have made a great difference to the lives of the inhabitants, giving more employment other than agricultural labouring, such as coachmen, gardeners, and indoor servants. It also generated more traffic, as visitors from outside the parish arrived and left, and the resident families visited each other. Transport being in the main by horse, the blacksmiths and farriers must have benefited considerably. All these families helped in the improvement of the church and in the building of the new school.

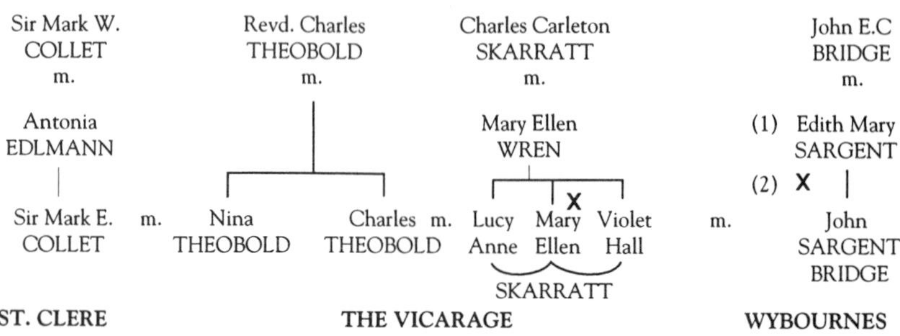

National Census 1891

A comparison between the national census returns of 1881 and 1891 shows that there was an increase of one hundred and seventy-eight in the population and of about fifty houses during the decade. It is not easy to identify these new houses because the enumerators *(Edward J. Cope in 1881 and Alfred G. Jordan in 1891 - both schoolmasters)* used different routes round the parish when making their notes. However, it is probable that the more recent houses included Yew Tree Cottages, Landway Cottages *(35-45, West End)*, Nos. 51 and 53, West End; Stone Cottages at Heverham; Dilwyn; Downlands; and Cob Tree Down on Pilgrims Way; Beechy Lees; the Schoolhouse; Nos 79 to 85, West End; and about twenty-five cottages in Noah's Ark.

Another new house was called South View, built in the field next to Dippers Hall. Both are shown as occupied, the first by John Goldney and the Hall by two separate families. Although Mr. Goldney called his new house South View it later became known as Dippers Hall, probably when the old house was demolished. On old maps South View was shown as being some way further from the road than Dippers Hall, which stood approximately where White Lodge is now.

There was quite a difference in the occupants of the Vicarage *(now the Youth Hostel)*. Instead of a predominantly female household consisting of the Revd. George Bridges Lewis and his wife and four daughters looked after by a cook and two housemaids, there was now a bachelor establishment including the Revd. Thomas Carleton Skarratt, his brother Sydney, Mr. Robert M. Turnbull, and a butler, all looked after by a housekeeper and two domestic servants. Mr. Turnbull was later succeeded in 1892 as curate by Mr. C.A.M. Smith, who does not seem to have lived at the Vicarage. Some six years later the Revd. R.H. Benson occupied two rooms at the Vicarage while he was a curate in 1897 and 1898.

Many of the families who had been most prominent, both numerically and in their public service, had either died or moved away since 1881, including the Brownings, Assisters, Cawstons, Crowhursts, Jeffreys, Knells, Larkings, Pryers, Rudgards and Wigzells.

Church Enlargement And The 1890s

When the Revd. T.C. Skarratt decided to build a north aisle on the church, he found that quite a number of local residents were prepared to subscribe towards the cost. He commissioned a local architect, Thomas Graham *(later Sir Graham)* Jackson to undertake the work. The Skarratts and the Jacksons were probably well known to each other. The architect's sister, Emily, is remembered still as the donor of what was for many years known as the Emily Jackson Wing of Sevenoaks Hospital. In the X-Ray Department of the hospital is a plaque commemorating a gift by the Vicar's sister, Daisy. The inscription reads:- "The first X-Ray apparatus in use in this hospital was presented by Daisy Tennant in January 1909 in memory of her brother the Rev. Thomas Carleton Skarratt for nineteen years Vicar of Kemsing".

While the north aisle was being built, from November 1890 to May 1891, the Vicar had permission from the Archdeacon to hold services in the schoolroom. Men who worked on the building were not all from the village, and those who came from other places were deemed to be "foreigners" by the villagers. They found lodgings here, including Mr. Edwin Long, the Clerk of the Works, who stayed with Mr. Frederick Wagstaff in No. 1 St. Edith's Cottages.

In their spare time, some of the stonemasons made gifts like ornaments, picture frames, etc. for their hosts out of discarded pieces of stone. The flints used in the construction of the walls, were collected from the hill above by local women, carrying them down in baskets, to be delivered to two men who worked in the churchyard at knapping them into shape for the masons to build into the face of the walls. For this task they used special knapping hammers and wore wire mesh goggles to protect their eyes.

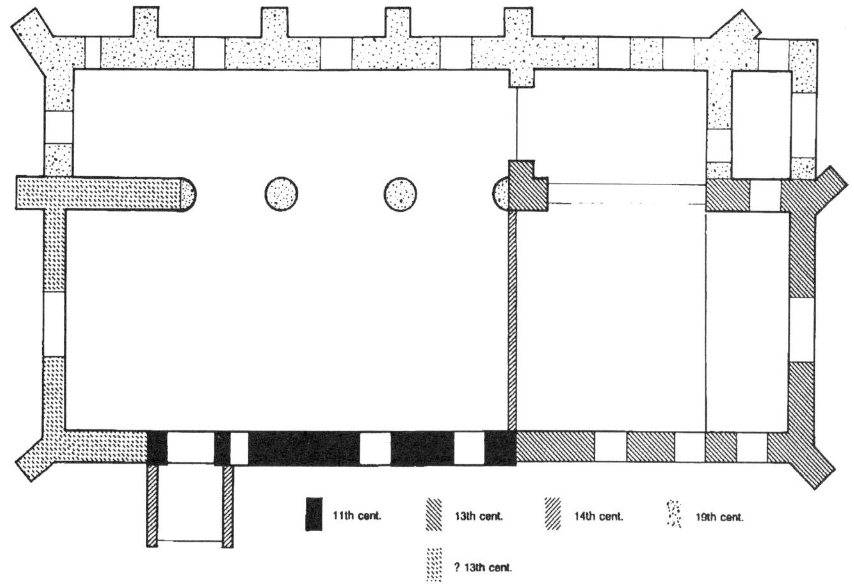

Plan of St. Mary's Church

It is believed that the pieces of old glass seen today in a jumble in the old frame in the north wall were recovered when the footings for the aisle were being dug. They are of both 14th and 15th century glass and form part of the old windows which were broken out in 1826. Coloured glass was put into the new small window over the Porch in 1893 by Mr. W.E.A. Schwenk in memory of his sister, Edith. Mr. Schwenk was a personal friend of the Revd. T.C. Skarratt, who marked this friendship by leaving to Mr. Schwenk in his will a diamond tie-pin and £100. The picture is of St. Edith as a Saxon Princess, and was made at the works of James Powell, which became the Whitechapel Glass Company. Powells employed many well known artists, and it is possible that this window was the work of a member of the Pre-Raphaelite Brotherhood. Unfortunately, the firm's records, held in the Victoria and Albert Museum, do not include those for the year 1892/93.

The total cost of the new aisle and the vestries amounted to £3,436, of which Mr. Barclay Field contributed £1,191 and Sir Mark Collet £1,155. The plaster ceiling of the chancel was removed and the rafters revealed. A plaster panel filling the space over the screen was also removed, and the floor of the chancel was re-laid with black and white tiles. The pews throughout the church were replaced by new oak pews made in the St. Clere workshops. Some of the redundant pews of the 1870 restoration were sold off to parishioners. Mr. J. Whitehead, the carpenter at St. Clere, made an oak platform for use at the font. He left an inscription on the underside to the effect that it had been made in time for the re-opening of the church on 19th May 1891. In the following year an oak screen was erected between the north aisle and the choir vestry. Alterations were needed to the siting of some of the old gravestones. One which was originally in the centre of the nave was moved from near the font to its present position under the sedilia in the sanctuary. The half-brass to Thomas de Hop was also moved to the sanctuary, together with the stone slab now just to the east of it. Two years after the restoration of the rood loft over the screen in 1894, Sir Mark Collet had a new pulpit installed at the south end of the screen where it still stands. It was designed by Comper and the carved figures which adorn its walls were the gift of the Vicar's sisters. The old pulpit had been on the north end of the screen until 1891, when it was moved to the east end of the new aisle, next to the vestry door.

At this period the village was served by several trades-people, including Charles Martin *(grocer)*; William H. Foster *(grocer and draper at Noah's Ark)*; Arthur Long *(grocer)*; James Reeves *(blacksmith at Heverham)*; Amos Wren and Albert King *(butchers)*; and Joseph S. Geering *(glazier)*.

Under the Local Government Act of 1894 Easter Vestries ceased to have their civic powers to raise rates and to appoint Overseers and Waywardens. These duties were now to be undertaken by the new Parish Council. The first meeting of this body in Kemsing was held on 4th December 1894, possibly at the school. It was attended by Messrs. Allan Botting, William E. Alexander, J. Cordery, T. Johnson, J.P., William H. Foster, Amon Wren, Frederick Waghorn, and the first chairman Mr. J.C.E. Bridge. Mr Alfred G. Jordan, the schoolmaster, was appointed clerk to the council. In 1895 the council began to discuss the five main topics that would occupy most of their time during the following fifteen to twenty years, and are still under discussion today. They were street lighting; footpaths; the well area; water supply and sanitation; and recreational accommodation. For the latter several sites were considered, including Long Mead, Christmas Bush, and Hackett's Field, but eventually Cricketting Field was leased. This area was located in the angle between Pilgrims Way and Five Acre Lane, now occupied by Fairmont and Brushwood Cottage. In December 1895 the new Parish Council became the owners of the well area. This small piece of land, described as "waste", had been a part of the Manor of Kemsing, and it was presented to the village by Lord Sackville. It was made safer two years later by the erection of a fence all round, a move possibly motivated by the fact that some

time earlier a man had been found drowned in the well. He was George Danes, of no fixed abode, who had been employed by Mr. Stonham at Dynes Farm. He overbalanced while bending to fill a kettle with water. Emma Holmden found him when she went to draw water that morning. She alerted the postman and he sent her to get help from Mr. Mills, the publican at The Bell Inn, who pulled the man out. The well caused the Parish Council more worries later on. Firstly the top had to be covered by an iron grille made by the blacksmith at Heverham, because there had been several cases of children having to be rescued in previous years. And in 1898 a drought caused the stream and the well to run dry. Deepening the well had no effect and the pump beside it also failed to work. This state of affairs was reflected in 1992, when the stream began to flow again after a period of drought which had caused it to dry up for some four years. Also in 1898 the pond by the old school in St. Edith's Road dried up, so it was filled in. The Council's right to fence in the well area was challenged by Jesse Young, who erected two posts close to the well for his own purposes, although what those purposes were is not known. The argument went on for months.

The following year there was water in the well and the Mid Kent Water Company piped supplies from the well down to Noah's Ark. Some of the inhabitants there, however, misused the facility and it was withdrawn.

Two more proposals were discussed by the Parish Council, neither of which bore fruit. The first was an offer by the Mid Kent Gas Company to bring gas into the village, and the other was a suggestion that the railway station should be moved to Noah's Ark bridge. At the church more changes were made. In 1894 the Vicar erected the lychgate at the east end of the churchyard, complete with a central post on which to rest the coffin before entering the burial area. This was removed in the 1970s. Two copper lamp holders, previously hanging in the chancel, were moved into the nave and joined by a third, made to match. The first of these lamps is said to have been brought back by Mr. Skarratt from a visit to Venice.

The little organ in the chancel was replaced in 1896 by one made by Auguste Gern, a French organ builder. It cost about £600, which was raised by public subscription. To accommodate the pipes a floor was inserted over the choir vestry. This extended two or three feet into the aisle, forming a ledge on which some of the pipes were arranged to fill the gap of the arch. These were decorated and held in place by two bands of highly carved oak, making an attractive finish to the east end of the aisle.

In 1895 Beechy Lees was unoccupied but the other large houses were lived in by the Rudgards at Crowdleham, the Corderys at Crowdleham Cottage, the Alexanders at The Box House, the Covells at St. Edith's Farm, the Goldneys at Dippers or South View, John Underwood at Fair View on the Pilgrims Way, and Miss Goose at West House.

An indenture dated 28th December 1900, concerned with Crowdleham Cottage, contained a schedule listing many properties in Kemsing and Seal owned by the Rogers family of Riverhill House, Sevenoaks. In that year Col. John Middleton Rogers still owned Crowdleham Cottage, which his grandfather had acquired in about 1862. He also owned St. Edith's Farmhouse with fifty-one acres, occupied by Mr. Covell; Crowdleham Farm; Malthouses; and four hundred and one acres of St. Edith's Farm, occupied by Mr. G.H. Field of Beechy Lees; Crowdleham House and nineteen acres occupied by Mr. William Rudgard; West House, rented by the Revd. T.C. Skarratt; Stonepitts and a hundred and eighty-five acres, occupied by Mr. Philip Symons; Noah's Ark and eight acres occupied by Mr. Amon Wren; and various cottages and fields, totalling eighty-four acres and let to various tenants, including the villagers who rented the allotments on Croft Field, West End, on which Nos. 6 to 32 West End now stand.

In 1897, at the time of Queen Victoria's Diamond Jubilee the occupier of St. Edith's Farm, Mr. Covell, applied to the Parish Council for permission to divert a footpath which ran from the St. Edith Road to the Heverham Road, and passed very close to his living room windows. He was permitted to make the change on condition that he fenced the new path adequately. This he did, using iron railings with a gate at each end. The Queen's Jubilee was celebrated by the opening of this new path, still called Jubilee Footpath, by children marching up and down from end to end, blowing trumpets and banging drums.

BENSON AND COMPER

Among the many visitors to the Vicarage in Mr. Skarratt's time were two men who were destined to become well known nationally. One was the Revd. Robert Hugh Benson, a son of the Archbishop of Canterbury, and younger brother of the writers A.C. and E.F. Benson. He attended one of the retreats at Kemsing organised by the Vicar, and he was impressed by the experience. After being ordained, he took up residence in the Vicarage, and acted as curate at Kemsing for some two years. He was a prolific writer, and he has described how beautiful it was living there with the church just at the end of the garden. He enjoyed working with children and wrote and produced plays for them to perform. In gratitude they taught him to ride a bicycle up and down the High Street. While living at the Vicarage he made the acquaintance of Mr. Alexander Marshall, the organist, and his son Frank. With the latter he planned to publish a parish magazine, but there is no evidence that this venture materialised. He eventually joined the Roman Catholic Church and became Monsignor Benson before his death at the early age of forty-two.

The second notable visitor was a young architect called John Ninian Comper, whom the Vicar commissioned to carry out the restoration and redecoration of the chancel. Work began about 1896, and was completed by the addition of the figures on the screen in 1902. Comper based much of his style on the usages of the Eastern Orthodox Church. He was much admired for his work, which can be seen in numerous cathedrals and churches throughout the country: e.g. Wymondham Abbey, Norfolk; All Saints Convent, London Colney, Herts; St. Mary's, Wellingborough, Northants; and Wimborne St. Giles, Dorset. Of his time at the Vicarage, he has written of the beauty of the garden and of the interesting fellow guests. The latter included a French gentleman called De Larpent who was an expert in and authority on the works of William Shakespeare. The decoration of the chancel included oak wainscot panelling which was the gift of the Vicar and his brother and sisters in memory of their parents, Charles who died in 1900, and Mary Ellen who died in 1901. These panels all include carvings of the squirrels that appear in the Skarratt coat of arms. Above them, he put the coats of arms of many people who had connections with Kemsing in some way, such as the Sackvilles of Knole, the Collets of St. Clere, the Bunces of Crowdleham, the Bridges of Wybournes, the Skarratts and the Theobalds. The arms of Rochester and Canterbury are included together with that of St. Thomas of Canterbury, probably in reference to the Vicar's first Christian name. The addition of the rood figures involved adding a beam on which to erect them, and when fitting this beam the ends of the original rood beam were discovered embedded in the walls. The Royal coat of arms below the figures are those of

Edward VII in whose reign the work was finished. They appear to have no significance other than as a mark of respect to the Monarch as head of the Church of England. However, a Coronation Memorial Fund was opened in 1902 with £25 from the Parish Council, and in 1904 Mr. Edwards, Secretary to the Fund Committee, used money "left over" to buy fire fighting equipment. On what then, was the bulk of the fund spent? Could it have been this Royal Coat of Arms?

After the completion of the chancel decoration, Comper continued to add to the treasures of the Church. In 1902, he designed the east window which was a tribute from the Vicar to the memory of his mother. The inscription reads: "To the best of mothers, Mary Ellen Skarratt, died 1902, from her son Carleton". To enable this window to be placed in the east wall of the church, the Crucifixion window given by the Revd. G.B. Lewis had to be moved into the south wall of the chancel. This move may have been prompted by Comper's following of the Eastern style which used representations of Christ in Majesty rather than the Crucifixion. Moreover, having erected the Crucifix on the screen, to have a second Crucifix in the east window would have seemed to him to have been repetitive.

Another Comper window was inserted into the hitherto blank north wall of the sanctuary, which had formerly held the memorials and hatchment of the Bunce family. This window was a tribute from the Vicar to the memory of a cousin, Elizabeth R. Hall, who died in Australia in 1878.

After the death of the Vicar, his family and friends were determined that his memory should be kept, for they commissioned Comper to design two windows, and a brass memorial set in the floor of the chancel. The first window, from his family, is in the west wall, and depicts the Annunciation by the Angel Gabriel to the Virgin Mary. This is the only Comper window in Kemsing which bears his signature, which was a strawberry leaf, flower, and berry. The second window, in the north aisle, and given by his friends, is of two lights. In one, the figure of St. Thomas of Canterbury evidently refers again to the Vicar's Christian name, and in the other the figure of St. Richard of Chichester probably refers to his second Christian name, because there was once a Bishop of Chichester whose name was Carleton. Finally, in 1914, Comper designed the oak lectern mentioned earlier.

St. Clere

Mention of St. Clere having been made from time to time it is perhaps appropriate to bring its story up to date here.

During the latter half of the 17th century, conditions at St. Clere had deteriorated considerably. Sir John Sidley, the second baronet, left the property to his son, Sir Isaac and he, in turn to his son Sir Charles. The latter was somewhat feebleminded and let the estate become almost derelict. He lived in one or two rooms of the house and an inventory taken after the death of Sir John in 1673 shows that even then the house was very sparsely furnished. In the main "chamber" were a four-poster bed, a chair, a couch, two stools and a chest of drawers containing four tablecloths, three dozen napkins, some towels and four pairs of old sheets. The "gilt leather chamber" held another bed, with a chair and a table. The withdrawing room had just a bedstead and a stove. The wainscote chamber held eight chairs and four stools, another bedstead and a chest of drawers, some chimney furniture and some other bits and pieces.

Sir Charles was unmarried and lived a lonely and frugal life in these large and mostly bare rooms until his death in 1702. His title was inherited by his uncle John but Sir Charles left the house and the property round it to Sir John's son, George, and after him to George's brothers. There were large debts to be repaid and the house was in considerable need of repair, but George was not rich. He was married and had six children and he depended almost entirely on his father for financial support. The answer seemed to be to sell the house, but the terms of the will made this legally difficult. After a great deal of negotiation, the will was set aside, and the house sold, the debts paid off, and George and his family provided for. The purchaser of the house was William Evelyn, the great-nephew of John Evelyn the diarist.

He took over in about 1719 and found that not only was the interior in bad condition but the exterior and indeed the structure of the house was in a deplorable state. The rafters of the roof were rotten at the ends, and these had to be shortened and the ends disguised by the provision of a parapet around the roof. Rainwater gutters and pipes were renewed and marked with the initials WE and the date 1720. Inside the house, the walls were covered by pine panelling. The existing staircase was removed and a new one built, wide enough to accommodate the fashionable hooped dresses of the ladies of the day, and probably for the same reason the south entrance passage was widened.

Because St. Clere was still in the parish of Ightham the Evelyns improved the road to that village but they also opened a new one running westwards to Wildernesse Avenue giving access to the Pilgrims Way to the north and Heverham to the south.

The last of the Evelyn family to own St. Clere was the Revd. Edmund Boscawen Evelyn, whose grandfather William Evelyn was half-brother to Fanny Boscawen, the noted eighteenth century bluestocking. She had often stayed at St. Clere where she enjoyed the peace and tranquillity and the extensive views over the Kentish countryside. Mr. Boscawen Evelyn lived at Yaldham Manor and St. Clere was occupied in 1841 by William Bartlett, a farmer who was employed as caretaker. By 1851 he was a widower of sixty with a foster daughter, Elizabeth Knight, aged twenty living with him.

The tenant of Lower St. Clere in 1841 was Thomas Lockyer, who farmed the land for the Evelyn family. His household consisted of his wife, Mary, and children Alfred, Marie and Emma, and they employed a servant and three agricultural labourers. In 1851 this house had become the home of Matthew Rogers who farmed three hundred acres. He was twenty-eight in 1851, when he moved into the house with his wife Lucy and son Matthew. They employed a house servant, a nurse, a cowman, a waggoner, and an odd-man. All apart from the nurse were in their twenties.

Great changes were made in 1859, when the Revd. John Ogle, a forty-eight year old schoolmaster from Marylebone, moved into Lower St. Clere with his wife and nine children, and opened up the big house as a boarding school for boys, of whom there were fifty-one in 1861, aged from six to nineteen. The teaching staff included tutors in English and Mathematics, Classics and Mathematics, and French, and there was also a Governess. There were seventeen domestic servants, only two of whom were local so Mr and Mrs Ogle must have brought the whole staff from Marylebone. Mr. Ogle was listed as a voter for Kemsing in 1874, still living at Lower St. Clere but he was soon to move to Sevenoaks where he re-established his academy for boys.

When this happened, Mr. Evelyn sold the St. Clere Estate to Mr. M.W. Collet, Governor of the Bank of England. This change had a marked effect on the village of Kemsing. St. Clere was at that time in the parish of Ightham but Mr. Collet decided to adopt Kemsing rather than Ightham as his parish. He opened a new drive from the house to Heverham and Kemsing, and became a churchwarden at St. Mary's Church. By a series of purchases of small parcels of land adjacent to his property, he increased the total size of the estate considerably. He received a baronetcy in 1889 and revived an old tradition whereby wives of baronets were entitled to be called "Dame". Hereafter his wife was addressed as either Lady

Collet or Dame Antonia Collet. The wife of his son, the second Sir Mark, also enjoyed this title, when he inherited the baronetcy.

Sir Mark and Lady Collet *(his second wife, Violet nee Edlmann)* left Kemsing to live in the Isle of Man in 1935, and after that his nephew Montagu *(later Lord)* Norman lived in St. Clere. He died in 1950 and his nephew Brigadier H.R. Norman inherited the estate. The present owner, Mr Ronnie Norman, Kent County Councillor, has lived at St. Clere since his father's death in 1979.

Chapter 11
Edwardian Days And The Great War

The twentieth century began in the shadow of the wars in South Africa and on Sunday the 4th January 1900, the church collections were sent to the Soldiers Fund by the Queen's command. Other than that the people of Kemsing were not much affected by national events and were at the beginning of a decade of peace covering the reign of King Edward VII. But although most villagers went about their daily work with little haste or worry, changes were being made. Queen Victoria's death and funeral and the coronation of King Edward VII were no doubt marked by school holidays and perhaps by other events in the village of which no record has been left.

The Eleventh National Census held in 1901 showed a small rise of thirty-three in the population making a total of six hundred and forty-four. They occupied a hundred and thirty-seven houses which was twelve more than in 1891. These twelve included St. Edith's View which was erected in 1893 by Mr. Barclay Field for the accommodation of the church verger. The first of these was Mr. John Williams, who was eventually succeeded by George Williams in 1916 and Mr. H.J. Wise, who was Verger from 1918 to 1928.

The first motor car to be observed in the village bore the registration number FN 49. It was seen in 1900 by the eight year old Alice Wells of Noah's Ark, standing outside the Box House. What make of car it was and who was the intrepid traveller she did not know.

In 1901 the Vicar's mother, Mary Ellen Skarratt, died and was buried in the churchyard beside her husband who had died the year before. Over their grave was erected the largest monument to be seen in Kemsing, which must have been very impressive to the local people. A few years later another impressive gravestone was put up close by but of a very different design. Whereas the Skarratt grave held a very tall cross of a vaguely Celtic design the grave of Sir Mark W. Collet took the form of a table tomb supported on four columns, and very elaborately decorated to the design of Henry Wilson of Platt. *(This tomb was twice vandalised; in the 1980s, when the bronze plaque on the top was removed, and in 1991 when the four supporting columns were stolen).*

Other changes were taking place. Two of these were occasioned by house fires. The first destroyed some cottages which occupied the space between The Bell Inn and the Well. They were of wood with thatched roofs and no doubt burnt easily. The second fire was soon after, if not the following day, as some reports have it, and it was at Wybournes, the old house which was the home of Mr and Mr Bridge and family. In both these cases the local Fire Brigade were called out but were unable to cope owing to the lack of water, in spite of the fact that Fire Hydrants had been installed in the village in 1901. One eye-witness to this second fire was a young lad Gershom Williams, who was a tea boy working at Beechy Lees. When smoke was observed in the direction of the village his foreman told him to get on his bicycle and locate the fire. By the time that he got there the boy saw smoke and flames coming from the windows on the street side of the house. The effect of this fire was the removal from the parish of the Bridge family who left the ruined house. Some two or three years later Major Arthur Pearson Davison, the son of the Rt. Hon. John Robert Davison, QC., M.P., who was the Judge Advocate General, bought the garden and the ruins of Wybournes.

He intended to build himself a house there as Underriver House, which he had inherited from his father, was on a long lease. As the purchase included some eighteen acres of land he was able to build higher up the slope. While building was in progress the family stayed at The Box House. The new building was also called Wybournes although, as it was of red brick, it was known locally for some years as The Red House. Major and Mrs. Davison had five daughters and one son. The youngest daughter Elizabeth was born at Kemsing. The fourth daughter, Patricia, wrote a very interesting descriptive account of life at Wybournes in the years 1905 to 1918. This gives a clear picture of their family life and also their social life, mentioning "gentry" of the period, such as the Sackvilles at Knole, the Collets at St. Clere, the Marshams at Crowdleham and the Stewarts at the Vicarage. For some years the children were not encouraged to make friends of the village children, but after the War of 1914-18 the two youngest girls were allowed to join the Girl Guide Company, where they were delighted to make new friends. An older sister served throughout the war as a V.A.D. nurse at the hospital in the village hall.

Another change had been made by the death in 1905 of Sir Mark W. Collet when Sir Mark E. Collet inherited St. Clere. Dame Antonia Collet caused a memorial window to be erected in memory of Sir Mark. It was set in the old stone three light frame over the pulpit in place of the earlier window of much simpler design, which Mrs. Margaret Smith had provided as a memorial to her brother, George Turner. The latter is now remembered by a wall plaque in the north aisle. The new window was designed by Henry Wilson and made by Christopher Whall and his daughter. It depicts the Ascension and bears facial portraits in the figures of Moses, Christ and Elijah. The last named was of Sir William Hicks-Beach *(later Lord St.Aldwyn)* who was Chancellor of the Exchequer when Sir Mark was Governor of The Bank of England.

Further changes were made by the death of the Vicar in 1908. This meant that the Skarratt family left the village. The new Vicar was the Revd. Edward H. Stewart who was inducted on the 20th January, 1909. The Vicarage was no longer a bachelor establishment since Mr. and Mrs. Stewart had two daughters, Hilda and Eileen, and a son Henry.

The Parish Council had two or three problems to deal with at this time. In 1902 the Darent Valley Sewerage System could have been linked to the village but the Council voted against this as they did when the Sevenoaks Rural District Council planned to build an isolation hospital for small pox cases in Kemsing. This is interesting because there was a great deal of sickness in the village at the time and after an outbreak of diphtheria moves were made to have the water supply examined. In 1908 it was suggested that a Telephone Exchange might be introduced in Kemsing, but this was turned down. They also made application to Sevenoaks for a separate Polling Station in Kemsing but this was not allowed.

By this time mains water became available to some houses, but many owners were slow to have it connected.

A Post Office telegraph office was opened in Kemsing and guarantors had to be found. The first of these were in 1903 Sir Mark W. Collet, the Revd. T.C. Skarratt and Messrs. W. E Alexander, J.E.C. Bridge, T. Goldney, H. Avery and A.G. Jordan. It was then possible to send telegrams from the Post Office instead of from the station. The Post Office was by this time situated in Clement House in the High Street. Andrew Holden who had been postmaster since 1872 had run the business from his grandfather's cottage close to the old blacksmith's forge but when his uncle, Hezro Holden, the blacksmith, died leaving property to several nephews and nieces, Andrew negotiated with his cousins and was able to purchase Clement House. He moved the Post Office into one of the front rooms, which he converted into a shop by adding a bay window and a separate entrance.

The village was lucky enough to receive many donations and gifts. Money was given in large quantities to the church by the Dowager Lady Collet, Miss Waring of Crowdleham Cottage, and Miss Edlmann of Chantry Cottage, Miss D. Skarratt, Sir Mark E. Collet, the Revd. H. Stewart, and Mr. John Covell of St. Edith's Farm. A singing gallery was erected over the chancel in 1908 by Sir Mark Collet in memory of his father. A silver gilt chalice and paten were donated by Miss Daisy Skarratt; a pair of silver gilt cruets were given by the communicants of St. Mary's in memory of Mr. Skarratt who had died in September. It was now deemed necessary to have a safe in which to store some of these treasures, and one was purchased at a cost of £7.4s.2d.

Calm Days Before The Great War

The appearance of the village was greatly altered in the first few years of the reign of King George V. His coronation in 1911 was marked by the erection of a horse trough in the bank behind the well area. This was accepted on 31st January by the Parish Council as a gift from the Coronation Memorial Committee, and was connected to the main water supply by the Mid Kent Water Company.

Sir Mark Collet had offered in 1910 to give a village hall, and in March 1911, Messrs. Style and Winch, the brewers, sold part of the orchard to the east of The Wheatsheaf to him as a site for the hall. Mr. Godfrey Pinkerton was the architect commissioned to design the hall, which was to include a Men's Institute and a caretaker's house. The work went ahead rapidly, and by August of that year the Parish Council were able to hold a meeting there. Sir Mark charged the Council a rent of one horse bean per annum. A horse bean is said to be a local name for a broad bean.

The main hall was fitted with a stage but had no exit at the east end. The foyer was incorporated into the hall in 1913 for the purpose of rifle shooting, the targets being up on the stage, and the butts behind the bar. Sir Mark prepared plans for future extensions, such as a kitchen, a green room, and a larger Working Men's Club. These plans were used in 1926 when a kitchen and green room were added.

In 1968 the Working Men's Club was extended eastwards, and in 1978, when the new Small Hall was built, the old kitchen and green room were amalgamated with the Working Men's Club and a new kitchen and green room, together with new toilets, were built joining the main hall.

Behind the caretaker's cottage was a bath house available to villagers on certain conditions, and there was also a shed for housing some of the fire-fighting equipment.

This large complex altered the appearance of the High Street considerably, and the north end of St. Edith's Road was also extensively altered in 1912 when the Old Parsonage house, known as the Ivy House because it was completely smothered in ivy, was demolished. It had been occupied in the past few years by George and Mary Ann Bowyer, who used one of the rooms as a shop, selling to the children sweets and, in due season and more memorably, fireworks. The site was then developed as a row of four houses given the name of Vicarage Cottages. At the same time, the old school house was demolished, and on the site a pair of cottages, appropriately named School Cottages, was erected.

In the church several new features appeared just before the war, including the two windows in memory of Mr. Skarratt mentioned earlier, and a brass set into the chancel floor, designed by Ninian Comper, showing the late vicar in sacramental vestments, with his family coat of arms above the head.

In the north aisle, a small chapel was created at the east end by placing a small altar in front of the oak screen. This chapel was dedicated to All Saints by Bishop Harmer in 1913. After the Great War it became a war memorial chapel by painting the figures of St. George and St. Michael and the names of the fallen on the panels behind the altar. This work was probably by Comper for riddle curtains were incorporated in the design hanging from wrought iron brackets. The gold fleur-de-lys on the dark blue ground of these curtains were reminiscent of Comper's style. The chapel was dismantled in 1965 and restored in 1984, but the riddle curtains were removed altogether.

Also at this time, probably in 1913, six four-candle sconces were acquired from Otford Church, while two more were given to Woodlands and West Kingsdown churches. These two eventually hung in Woodlands Church, but were stolen in May 1977. The chancel furniture, which had been altered several times in the previous forty years, was finally changed into the arrangement of stalls as they are now. This was done at the expense of the vicar, the Revd. E.H. Stewart, in 1913.

The Post Office in Clement House became a telephone exchange in the Brighton telephone district with fifty lines in 1913. It was closed in 1927 when subscribers were transferred to the exchange at Seal.

This Strange Thing In The Sky

After the first successful crossing of the Channel in 1909 by an aeroplane piloted by Bleriot, a young American of French descent called John Moisant made the same flight the following year; accompanied, however, by a passenger. The latter was his mechanic, called Fileux. Moisant was aiming to reach London, from Paris. After circling the Eifel Tower, he made for Calais and from there began the crucial stage of the flight, which ended in a forced landing at Tilmanstone. After taking off from there, they flew on to Sittingbourne where they came down for petrol, and had to make another stop at Upchurch where the propeller was badly damaged on landing. A new propeller was soon fitted by the mechanic and two more unscheduled landings were followed by an intentional stop at Wrotham for petrol. Weather conditions caused the next stop which was in a field to the north of the Pilgrims Way at Heverham. It was on the 18th of August 1910 that little Percy Pyne, six years old and confined to his bedroom as he recovered from a childhood illness, witnessed the descent onto the hill at the back of Stone Cottages and called to his mother to "come and see this strange thing in the sky". The machine was badly damaged and the propeller again smashed. Fortunately a second propeller was available because Bleriot, the designer of the aeroplane, had arranged for it to be dispatched from Paris in case of necessity.

The plane had a wing-span of 28 feet and weighed 462 pounds, with three cylinders, 24 horse power and 1,200 rpm. The propeller was of two blades measuring six foot nine inches, and the maximum speed was 37 miles per hour. While the repairs were being carried out, the aeroplane became an object of interest to all in the neighbourhood and crowds came to look at it. Moisant's mascot, a little kitten, was given to seventeen year old Mathilda Burr of Malthouse Cottages, to look after. She was disappointed when the flight eventually continued with the kitten on board. Moisant himself was injured in the crash, and during the waiting period he was given hospitality by Sir Mark Collet at St. Clere. He was surprised upon arriving at the house to see over the roof of the squash court a model of a Bleriot type aeroplane such as the one that he had just crashed. This was in fact a wind-vane, erected in 1908. A ship in full sail formed the wind-vane of the old laundry on the opposite side of the courtyard, and the architect of the squash court thought to balance the ship, which represented the oldest form of transport, with the very latest thing - an aeroplane.

The repairs to the plane were carried out by Sir Mark's chauffeur, assisted by Mr. Chandler of Noah's Ark under a cover erected by Mr. James Reeves of Heverham, who collected twopence from each viewer. Mr. Chandler also made a model of the machine and exhibited it outside his house. On the first attempt at taking off from Kemsing, Moisant flew the machine round the house at St. Clere at the request of Lady Collet, who, being confined to the house, was anxious to see her first aeroplane. Unfortunately, in doing so he fouled an oak tree and delayed the take off from Kemsing again, until the sixth of September. After a forced landing between Otford and Shoreham, they finally reached the Crystal Palace, where the plane was put on view to the public.

KEMSING HOSPITAL AND THE WAR YEARS

At the outbreak of the War with Germany in August 1914, the Parish Council appointed Mr. Theophilus Riches as their representative on the local sub-committee for the relief of distress caused by the War, and a separate parish committee was also formed for immediate needs in the parish.

On 19th August the Parish Council met in the hall as usual but by 15th October it had been taken over by higher authority and converted into a VAD Hospital. Thereafter for the duration of hostilities, the Council met in the school. The first patients arrived in Kemsing a week after the opening. They were twenty Belgian soldiers. Miss Ada Waring was the Quartermaster, and she kept a record of admissions in a small notebook, adding comments occasionally on the appearance and character of the patient, the nature of his wounds, and sometimes his subsequent history. For instance, one man left the hospital in December 1914 to return to Calais, but when again wounded he came back to Kemsing with a label round his neck reading "To Sir Mark Collet". Patients were taken to London for discharge, but were usually sent back to

Calais or back to Kemsing for convalescing. Some remained in England as refugees and others went on to convalescent homes elsewhere in England.

Miss Waring also collected photographs and kept letters that she received from the men after their departure. One of them called Joseph Duntzer appears frequently as he married a Kemsing girl, Beatrice Chandler of Noah's Ark. He had been made a Chevalier of the Order of Leopold II, and was known to Kemsing people as the Chevalier.

The Commandant was Mrs. Mabel Wilkinson of Frankfield on Seal Chart. She was assisted by Miss Waring and two Asst. Quartermasters, Miss Boyle and Miss Lacey. The Quartermaster's Office was across the road in a tack room on the ground floor of what is now Little Wybournes. There were seventeen VAD Nurses, mostly members of Kemsing and local families such as the Davisons, the Riches, the Stewarts and the Wilkinsons. In addition there were over twenty-four trained nurses and seven helpers.

Mrs. Jordan, the Headmaster's wife, was one of the six cooks who were assisted by eight orderlies, of whom George Wren was the only civilian.

Throughout the war years the hospital was kept in touch with the village, because concerts were held frequently, and the walking wounded were always to be seen about the streets in their distinctive "hospital blue" uniforms.

Some one thousand and twenty-eight wounded soldiers were cared for from 1914 to the closing of the hospital in 1918. It was re-opened as the village hall on 11th January 1919 when a final concert was held.

The presence of these wounded soldiers in the parish and the exigencies of the War must have affected the activities of the villagers, and yet they seem to have carried on a fairly normal life. They tried to institute a bus service to Sevenoaks, but the North Kent Motor Bus Company could not find enough buses. New interests were encouraged by the formation of branches of national organisations. A branch of the Church of England Men's Society had been formed in 1912, and in January 1915 a special Men's

Service was held at the church, followed in March by one for women, who were mostly members of the Mothers Union branch which had been founded in Kemsing in 1912.

On 26th November 1915 a Women's Institute branch *(the first in Kent and the seventh in Britain)* was inaugurated and on 1st January 1916 the sixteen founder members held their first meeting with the Vicar's wife, Mrs. Stewart, as their President.

Sir Mark Collet and the Vicar were both present at the inaugural meeting, which was held at the Vicarage as the St. Edith Hall was occupied by the hospital. The first members included Mrs. King of No. 1 Vicarage Cottages; Mrs. Thom of Dynes Farm; Nurse Wallis of 4 Vicarage Cottages; Miss Blane, a lady's maid from Chantry Cottage; Mrs. Jordan of the School House; the two Miss Riches of Dilwyn, one of whom was a teacher; Mrs. Fenn, wife of the caretaker of the hall; Mrs. Nicholls, the wife of the head gardener at St. Clere; Mrs. Davidson of Heverham Farm; Mrs. Simmons of Pilgrims *(Hon. Treasurer)*; Mrs. Kerr of Dippers (Hon. Secretary); Miss Westmorland of 2 Vicarage Cottages; Miss Beeby of Cotfield, 35 West End, governess to the Stewart children; and Miss Ada C. Waring of Crowdleham Cottage.

As part of the drive for more food, the recreation ground *(Cricketing Field on the Pilgrims Way)* was ploughed up, and a Rat and Sparrow Club was formed. Bread was hard to get in Kemsing, owing to a certain bureaucracy in Sevenoaks.

Motorists were becoming more numerous and the trees round the well had to be cut back to make the turning into St. Edith's Road safer.

In 1917, with a view to returning to normal when the War was over, the proposal was made for the provision of twelve council houses. This eventuated in the building of Croft Cottages, 6 to 28 West End, in the 1920s. Their name derived from the fact that the field on which they were built was at one time called Randolph's Croft. This was the field where the men of Kemsing had formerly rented allotments from Mr. Rogers.

The ending of the War was marked by a special thanksgiving service on 11th November 1918, and on 6th July 1919 there was a day of national prayer for the signing of the Peace Treaty. Peace celebrations, in which several of the returned service men were able to participate, were held in the village on Saturday, 19th July, with sports and a children's tea in the afternoon, followed by a carnival procession and open-air concert in the evening, ending at 10.30 pm with fireworks on Green Hill. On the following Tuesday a supper for returned servicemen was held.

KEMSING.

Peace Celebrations, Sat. July 19th

Commencing at 1 o'clock sharp:

CHILDREN'S SPORTS, followed by
SPORTS for ELDER BOYS, GIRLS & ADULTS
CHILDREN'S TEA at 4, ADULTS at 5

CARNIVAL

Meet at West End at 7 p m.

ROUTE—Noah's Ark, Kemsing Station,
Heverham, Kemsing.

3 prizes for Best Decorated Vehicle (Horse or Motor)
3 ,, Best Decorated Bicycle
3 ,, Best Decorated Horse
3 ,, Best Costume.

It is hoped that everybody who can take part in above will do so.

On the return of the Procession, an
OPEN-AIR CONCERT
will take place in the Village.

10.30—FIREWORKS ON GREEN HILL.

It is particularly requested that all inhabitants will decorate their premises as much as possible on this occasion, also that NO Fireworks be discharged during the Carnival Procession.

Tuesday, July 22nd, at St. Edith's Hall,

SUPPER for RETURNED SOLDIERS,
at 6.30 for 7 o'clock (Wife or Mother also invited).
followed by SMOKING CONCERT open to all.

God Save the King.

KEMSING
KENT
CANTERBURY
PILGRIMS WAY

Chapter 12
Between The Wars

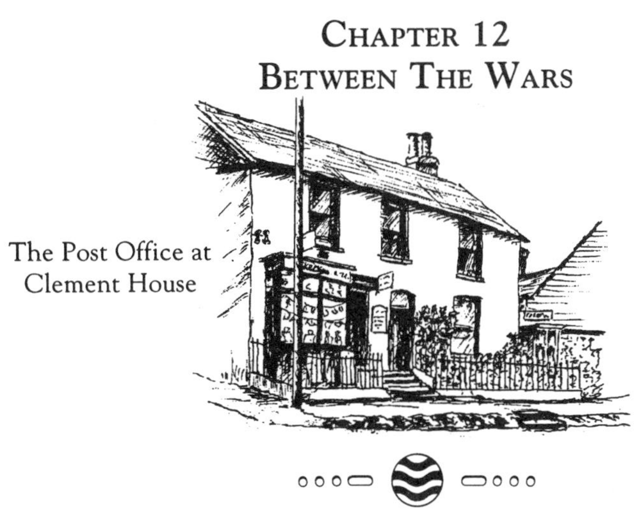
The Post Office at Clement House

The Nineteen-Twenties

After the first World War large areas of the parish were offered for sale by two estates. The first auction sale, held on the 23rd July 1919 at the Royal Crown Hotel in Sevenoaks, was of twenty-six lots of the Kemsing Estate offered by Lieutenant Colonel J.M. Rogers, DSO. The second, on the 10th September that year and again at the Royal Crown, was of fifty lots, comprising the Beechy Lees Estate. From the details published and from the maps accompanying the schedules, it is possible to form a picture of the parish at that time. Perhaps the item with the most lasting effect on the village was the sale of Church Field, which was next to the church and one-third of which was an orchard, to Sir Mark Collet, who had offered to present it to the parish as a Common Field. In view of this, the Parish Council discontinued their rental of the cricketing field and the pavilion there was given to the school for use as a garden shed.

There were five farms, all rented out. They were St. Edith's *(Mr. G.M. Davidson)*; Dynes *(Mr. W. Thom)*; Shorehill *(Mr. W.G. Smith)*; Cotman's Ash *(Mr. H. Booker)*; and Heverham *(Mr. G.M. Davidson)*.

Many areas were marked as prospective building sites. Had they been sold as such, Kemsing would have mushroomed into a large village, but there was little call for large housing estates and no new houses were built at that time.

By now the Women's Institute, having concentrated on war efforts for their first four years, were able to branch out into projects for the benefit of the parish. They founded a company of Girl Guides in 1922; ran a lending library based in the St. Edith Hall; started a tennis club; and made themselves responsible for providing refreshments for the men who had volunteered to work on the village War Memorial. As a site for the latter, Sir Mark Collet bought a piece of land near to The Bell Inn, and commissioned Mr. Godfrey Pinkerton to design the Memorial. Much voluntary work, mostly of the variety of levelling ground, mixing cement, laying bricks and so on, was done by the men of the village. The re-sited path between the well and The Bell was marked off by concrete posts made at St. Clere by George Miles and Alfred Haynes, and linked by iron chains also made at St. Clere.

The memorial was unveiled in 1921 by Lord Sackville in the presence of a large gathering at a Dedication Service conducted by the Archdeacon of Tonbridge assisted by the Vicar, the Revd. E.H. Stewart, and Mr. Simmonds, the leader of the Free Church in St. Edith Road. The service was followed by another for the dedication of the memorial in the church. Some forty ex-servicemen attended these services.

The summer of 1921 was unusually hot and dry, causing the death of the ancient yew tree that stood in front of the chancel of the church. This tree, some 1,300 years old, was cut down to its present height in 1925 by Mr. Harryman of the St. Clere Estate and it has been said that the actor, Henry Ainley, who was living at Seal Chart, came to watch this operation.

Sir Mark Collet's gift of the Common Field was much appreciated by the Football Club, who were too anxious to play on it; in spite of being warned that it was not yet fit to be used they did so, and in consequence one of them suffered an accident brought about by falling on flints. In continuation of his benefactions, Sir Mark gave another piece of land for an extension to the churchyard southwards. His architect, Mr. Pinkerton, bounded it with a crinkle-crankle wall which was built entirely by one man. This was Mr. Mungeow of Otford, who cycled daily to Kemsing from Otford in a bowler hat with his coat flying out behind him. He used to stop at The Wheatsheaf for a drink before starting work, and he also had his lunch there. This consisted of a couple of pounds of potatoes and a large steak, the latter being bought at the butcher's opposite, and cooked for him by Mrs. Small, the publican's wife. Sir Mark made it his practice to inspect the progress every day, and to make sure that "old Mungy" was well supplied with liquid refreshment.

Two newcomers who were to make their mark in the parish, for the next decade in one case, and the next three decades in the other, were the Revd. Ronald V. Bristow, who was appointed as curate by Mr. Stewart, and Mr. L.L. Lowing. Mr. Bristow lodged for a while in Ivy Farmhouse with Mr and Mrs. Jock Davidson. Upon the retirement of Mr. Stewart in 1924, Mr. Bristow was instituted as Vicar. Because the Vicarage *(Cleves)* was too large for him, arrangements were made for Chantry Cottage *(the present Vicarage)* which had been occupied by Sir Mark's relative, Miss S. Edlemann, until her death in 1920, to be enlarged and made into a new Vicarage. Mr. Bristow and his wife moved into it from Cleves in 1926.

Mr. Leonard Lowing was more fortunate in that he was able to move into a house straight away when he succeeded Mr. A.G. Jordan as Headmaster. The latter had retired a year or so before after thirty-six years of devoted service to the community as Headmaster, Parish Clerk, Asst. Overseer of the Poor, secretary of the Working Men's Club, and choirmaster. He went to live at Heverham.

In the event, Mr and Mrs. Lowing found that their accommodation was not so wonderful. The school, having been built in 1885, was in need of repair, and Mr. Lowing found himself teaching on wet days holding an umbrella over his desk. Sadly Mr Jordan did not live long to enjoy his retirement, but died in 1923. His widow Jane continued to serve the village in many ways for the next thirty years. She lived in Cotfield, now 35 West End.

Sir Mark Collet conveyed his gifts to the village by legal deeds of gift of the St. Edith Hall, and the Common Field. These now became the property and responsibility of the Parish Council. Byelaws for the Common Field, formulated and published in 1924, were adhered to until the Common Field, which has always been a great asset to the village, became a Charitable Trust in 1988.

Following upon the sale of the Beechy Lees Estate in 1919, the house itself was put on the market by the Field family and was eventually acquired by the Revd. Arthur Tooth. He was a clergyman who had experienced a period of imprisonment for his opinions on the subject of the wearing of vestments at the end of the nineteenth century. He founded a Sisterhood for Anglo-Catholic nuns at Woodside near Croydon, and when his property there was needed for development by the local council, he moved to Kemsing with a few of the remaining sisters. He also had a school for orphan boys, and as time went by, Beechy Lees, which he re-named Otford Court, became St. Michael's Preparatory School for the sons of the clergy and of serving officers overseas. He acted as warden, in which post he was succeeded by the brothers Blofeld. The Revd. Charles died in 1938 and was followed by the Revd. Thomas Guest Blofeld, who was warden until his death in 1964. He was buried in his brother's grave in Kemsing churchyard and his funeral was conducted by two bishops, those of Rochester and of Willesden. *(The latter, Dr. Graham Leonard, was chairman of the school governors. He became Bishop of Truro and then Bishop of London, and was a national figure during the debate on the ordination of women in 1992).*

In 1927 the Lyle family moved into Shorehill *(now called Otford Manor and before that Hildenborough Hall but also affectionately known as "Treacle Towers")*. This large house had taken six or seven years to build, employing nineteen Kemsing men.

The question of lighting for the village hall and for the church came up in 1926, when the kitchen was being added to the Hall. Mr. Oliver Lyle offered to supply electricity from his generator to both buildings. Arrangements were made for the supply to the hall to be paid for initially by Sir Mark Collet, who was to be reimbursed by the Parish Council after two years. This facility was maintained until 1961 and many people can remember the poles and wires coming down Side Hill from Shorehill to the hall. The offer to the church was not taken up because, as Mr. Lyle expected to go on to the mains in less than ten years, it was thought wise to accept an offer from the Sevenoaks and District Electricity Company to bring a cable as far as the lych gate for a very reasonable sum. The acquisition of a kitchen made it possible to hold cooking classes for girls of the village and the boys were able to take lessons in woodwork in there and in the Noah's Ark mission hut, under the instruction of a Mr. Woolley of Maidstone. These boys had also had, since Mr. Jordan's time, the advantage of taking lessons in gardening at the school, the instructor being Mr. Matthew Nicholls, head gardener at St. Clere.

Having moved into the new Vicarage Mr. Bristow's next move was on behalf of the youth of the village when he formed a troop of Boy Scouts in 1926. The initial membership of eight scouts and one scoutmaster increased within months to seventeen. Throughout his ministry, Mr. Bristow worked hard with the scouts, taking them on camping holidays, sometimes on the continent. Possibly inspired by Sir Mark Collet's great interest in St. Edith, he instituted the custom of processing to St. Edith's Well on or near to her Feast Day, the sixteenth of September. His friend, Miss Muriel Minter, designed and painted the St. Edith Banner for the first celebration. At some time, probably during the second World War, the custom fell into disuse, but it was revived in 1961 and has been observed ever since. Another painting of St. Edith took the form of a tympanum over the inner side of the entrance to the St. Edith Hall. This mural was designed by Miss E. Parker and painted by students at the Beckenham School of Art, who were awarded first prize in the Kent Schools Art Competition that year.

The winter of 1927/28 started very early, and Harvest Festival held on the 7th October was poorly attended as the early snow had damaged so much of the produce. By December the snow was three to four feet thick and even up to sixteen feet in some parts of the parish, isolating the village for a week.

Towards the end of this decade, village organisations began to flourish, and new ones were founded. The scout troop increased its membership and became the 6th Sevenoaks *(Kemsing Church)* Group. A Wolf Cub pack was started by Miss Peters.

The Women's Institute continued their benefactions to the parish by supplying seats to be placed on the Common Field. They campaigned for public conveniences to be built in the village but the Parish Council felt that there was no need for them, nor did they support a plea for street lighting. Six more iron seats were presented by the ex-servicemen's Society. As to sports, the original Kemsing Institute Football Club lost strength but the Kemsing United Football Club flourished.

Public telephones were installed by the well, at Noah's Ark and at Heverham, and Kemsing was declared a separate polling district in 1930 and became part of the Sevenoaks Rural District Council's area. At the church several changes were made. The first parish magazine was produced in 1929, being printed and published by the Vicar, Mr. Bristow, on his press in the vicarage, which he styled "The Chantry Press". To heat the church building a Grundy hot air service was installed. It served well for the next fifty years. The Vicarage was also enlarged at this time.

Several notable characters died including Andrew Holden, who had been postmaster since 1872; Mr. H.J. Wise, who had been verger for the last ten years; and Miss Mary Smith, who had taught at the school from 1890 to 1926.

It was a great shock to the village when in May 1926 Mr. Horace Avery, who had managed the butcher's shop in the High Street for twenty-seven years, hanged himself in the cellar of his house opposite the shop.

Among the houses built in this decade was Copperfield, which Mr. Gershom Williams erected for Mr. Bowes in 1920/21, in several acres of land stretching from West End to the Pilgrims Way. Meanwhile on the Pilgrims Way west of the junction with Childsbridge Lane, Mr. Thompkins built three double-fronted houses, together with several more at that end of Childsbridge Lane.

THE NINETEEN THIRTIES

In common with many other villages, Kemsing began to expand throughout the years leading up to the second World War. Two rows of shops were built, one in the West End and the other in Dynes Road. Council houses had already been built in West End, and more were built on the Pilgrims Way to accommodate residents of the Malthouse Cottages in Heverham Road. These cottages, which had housed seven families, had been condemned as unfit for habitation, but were later reconditioned and made into one house in 1938, by Mr. David Winch of the brewers Style and Winch, who employed Albert Swaisland as a caretaker. The seven tenant families were re-housed in the newly-built houses on the Pilgrims Way. The Malthouse was then bought by Sir Waldron Smithers, M.P, for his son.

The population of the parish was slowly increasing and in 1931 numbered nine hundred and fifteen, living in two hundred and twenty-two houses, which was seventy-two more than in 1921. This spread of housing had continued year by year, although since no census was taken in 1941 it is not certain how many dwellings were put up in the 1930s. The old cottages in the High Street east of Clement House were demolished and replaced by The Old Forge and the two "New Cottages". The blacksmith's forge, occupied by the Holden family since the early 1800s, was also removed. Considerable building went on in the west of the village where Mr. F. Jarvis put up four blocks of four houses each on the north side of Dynes Road. Also, in collaboration with Mr. Caldwell of Greystones, Childsbridge Lane, he began to build semi-detached houses on the south side of Dynes Road and in Oxenhill Road. Mr. Caldwell lighted these roads by installing several electric lamps, which were operated from his house.

Bungalows were beginning to appear in The Landway, which was then called "The Orchards" because the road ran between two plum and apple orchards. *(The new name, descriptive of any path giving access to agricultural land or to the back entrances to cottages, referred to the fact that this road was originally a track between two hop gardens)*. Other houses were built at the top of Childsbridge Lane, and in The Chase; along the Pilgrims Way on the north side between Chalky Lane and St. Michael's grounds; in Park Lane and in Greenlands Road.

Another development which might have altered the nature of the village was brought about when a motor-cycling club rented a field in Childsbridge Lane, opposite Child's Cottage, from Mr. W. Small of The Wheatsheaf. Complaints about the noise they made there encouraged them to move away to Brands Hatch, which was then a remote spot, where they made their circuits on grass and rough surfaces.

Until 1934, Kemsing Parish boundaries did not include any part of St. Clere, but they did include fifty acres at Ash, which were counted as "Kemsing Without". This anomaly was amended and the fifty acres went to Ash Parish and part of St. Clere was transferred from Ightham to Kemsing. Some of the larger houses changed hands. Wybournes had been sold in 1922 to Colonel R.E. Bevington by Mr. A.P. Davison; Mr. Burnett sold Crowdleham in 1929 to Mrs. M. Burrows; Nearly Corner *(once called The Gables)* was occupied by Miss E.M. Barnard, Sir Mark Collet's secretary, who was a devoted worker for the Free Church. Cleves *(the Y.H.A.)* was the home of Capt. Charles Boyle; and Dippers belonged to Mr. A.F. Jenkins, whilst Captain Oliver Lyle lived at Shorehill.

The school, which had ceased to be a Church of England School in 1927, needed more classrooms, and a new block was provided higher up the slope. In 1928 a playing field had been acquired. It was part of a parcel of agricultural land which originally belonged to Mr. John Thornton Rogers, but changed hands in 1919 when his Kemsing Estate was sold off. Strips of land on the north and south borders of the field became the sites of council houses - Pilgrims Way Cottages and Croft Cottages. Levelling work on the field began on the 5th June 1928, and was completed by the 15th July. The next year, on the 5th June, Sir Mark Collet and the Kent Education Committee architect, Major Robinson, visited the site to make plans for the new buildings, which were eventually begun on the 15th July 1930 and completed by Messrs. Banks and Sons on the 31st October. There was an official opening on the 23rd April 1931, attended by Mr. Nottidge vice-chairman of the K.E.C; Sir Mark Collet; Captain Cornwallis; Mr. Elgood, and the Revd. R.V. Bristow. The first major event held on the new playing field was the Sevenoaks and District school sports competition on the 10th June, 1931.

Mr. Bristow left the parish in 1931, and the next ten years saw no less than four new vicars being instituted. They were: the Revd. Harold T. Graham *(1931)*, the Revd. C.H. Freeman *(1935)*, the Revd. Vincent Macreth *(1936)*, and the Revd. A.E. Scipio *(1939)*. Mr. Graham appears to have made very little impact on the village. Mr. Freeman was a sick man and died in office. He was keen to encourage youth work and was a scouter. His only memorial is a pair of wooden candlesticks given to the church by his sister. In his time, the question of lighting the church by electricity was again raised but nothing was done. In the event, such lighting was installed in 1938, but not until after much, often acrimonious, discussion and argument between the Vicar, Mr. Macreth, and some members of the Parochial Church Council. This Council was now influenced by the views of some newcomers to the parish. The building of houses and bungalows designed to attract retired professional people led to a difference in attitudes, and some of the "old village" life began to be changed. The installation of electric light was financed by a house to house collection and a state of the fund chart was erected behind the horse trough so that people could see how it was progressing. A thanksgiving service was finally held on 21st February 1939.

Sir Mark Collet continued to help the village in 1935 by giving a further extension of the churchyard to the west of the 1922 extension. This time the boundary wall was not a continuation of the crinkle-crankle wall, but was equally interesting as the brickwork included a design of crosses. The coping was also ornamental. He also gave a chest to hold altar hangings, and had it fitted in the north aisle under the window which he had erected in the west wall in memory of his mother and of his wife. This window was designed by the Scottish artist Douglas Strachan.

1936 was the year of the three Kings. King George V's Jubilee had been celebrated in 1935 and marked in Kemsing by the planting of a roundel of trees in the Common Field. His death in 1936 and the accession of King Edward VIII were not marked in any special way, nor did the abdication crisis and the accession of King George VI arouse much local feeling. People here were more concerned with local matters, such as the ever recurring call for street lighting, and of the introduction of gas into the village. The latter was opposed by the Sevenoaks Rural District Council, who did propose some road improvements and some road naming. Thus The Orchards became The Landway, the Pilgrims Road the Pilgrims Way, and the western end of Heverham Road renamed High Street.

The Coronation of King George VI in May 1937 was marked by a special service in church and the erection of a flagstaff in the grounds of the St. Edith Hall. In the same month, the school children celebrated Empire Day on the 24th by giving a concert. The year 1937 saw the move of the Free Church from the little chapel in St. Edith's Road to a house in Dynes Road, and in 1938 a new private school for girls up to the age of eleven and boys up to seven, was opened by Mrs Baker at Russell House in The Chase. It was later removed to its present location in Station Road, Otford.

The Boyle family having moved away from the parish, Cleves became another private school, run by Miss Gladys Mary Brocklehurst and her friend Miss Edith Lang. By 1938 the school seems to have been under the tuition of a Mr and Mrs. Stevenson, who named it Langdown School. When war clouds began to gather after the Munich crisis they closed the school. What happened then is not clear, but the school continued to operate in Miss Lang's house next door, which was then called Langcroft. *(Now Queensmead)*. Some time soon after that the old vicarage, or Cleves, was acquired by the Youth Hostel Association.

Chapter 13
World War II And After

The War Years

All through 1938 and 1939 tension grew nationwide as war became more and more likely. In Kemsing the Parish Council made preparations for the provision of air raid shelters and they had already appointed air raid wardens in 1937. Trenches were dug in the school field, the Common Field, Dippers grounds, at Heverham, and south of The Chequers, the brickfields at Noah's Ark, between Dynes Road and Childsbridge Lane, and on the Pilgrims Way.

The Revd. A.E. Scipio had scarcely moved into the vicarage on the departure of Mr. Macreth when war was declared on the 3rd September 1939, and he had to face all the difficulties presented by war conditions. Many of the regular residents had to leave the parish and new ones arrived, including military and some evacuees from London. The latter were accommodated mainly in the houses in "the White City" *(a local name given to the Dynes Road and Oxenhill Road development because of the white chalk dust which settled on everything there in that hot summer)*. Others were billeted under the direction of Miss Mary Burrows on many families throughout the area.

In 1938 five hundred people had received gas masks in the

village hall. The air raid wardens protested at claims that the village was not prepared. In fact, a great deal had been done. The wardens were well organised with a centre at Chalkpit Cottage, to which they reported every incident that occurred. These included: the crash of a Hurricane on the railway at Noah's Ark; the arrival of some eight flying bombs; and numerous cases of incendiary bombs causing fires. To help the fire-fighters, the well area was flooded as a temporary water supply. Balloon sites were established along the West End, High Street, and Heverham Road, manned by RAF personnel and designed to prevent the flying bombs from reaching London. Members of the British Legion branch, which had been formed in 1938, and the Women's Section which was formed a year later helped wherever necessary.

The army was represented by No. 425 Bulkbreaking Platoon, Royal Army Service Corps, which supplied various camps in the Wrotham area. They moved into any vacant or unoccupied premises. Thus the Malthouse, recently renovated, became the Officers' Mess. St. Edith's Farmhouse was the quartermaster's stores and other ranks billets. There was a general store in the long barn which used to lie behind the house. The Sergeants' Mess was over one of the shops in the West End. Clement House and The Box House were also billets, and in the village hall there was a canteen for the troops.

The whole village was subject to a nightly curfew at eleven o'clock and dances and concerts had to terminate at half past ten, while Evensong on Sundays was celebrated at three in the afternoon, because of the blackout regulations.

The LDV *(Local Defence Volunteers, later the Home Guard)* trained at Wybournes, and at Pilgrim Cottage in Heavens Lane, off the Pilgrims Way. They had an outpost on top of Green Hill. Parades were held every Sunday morning.

The northern half of the Common Field was ploughed and farmed by Mr. Brooks of Seal, and as the lower half had trenches across it, children were given permission by the Kent Education Committee to use the school field out of school hours on condition that they were always supervised by adults. Some of the soldiers tried to create a football pitch on the Common Field by cutting lines in the turf, but this damage had to be repaired under the direction of one Lieutenant Alex Funston, who was well known in the parish for years after the war as he came to live in Ivy Farm House.

To interest the younger men and boys, a class of cadets was formed at the school and affiliated to the Royal West Kent Regiment. To make things easier for the civilian population, a cash and carry kitchen was set up in the Free Church, Dynes Road, which had just been built, and was formally opened in 1941. This was the first cash and carry in a rural area, but it did not survive more than a year because it was not sufficiently supported by local people. A clothing club was also formed, the trustees being the Vicar and members of St. Mary's Church and of the Free Church.

By 1944, plans were already being made for welcoming servicemen and women back to the village, and in February 1945, a circular letter went out signed by Miss Burrows, Mr. C.H. Brett, and Mr. L.B. Burtt, asking for contributions to a fund for welcome home parties. Several of these were held in the village hall in the first years after the war, and certificates marking the gratitude of the village to the recipients were given to each of the guests at these gatherings.

The 8th May, 1945 was the night which saw lights on again and many children who had never seen them before enjoyed the spectacle of the blaze of light afforded by Shorehill *(now Otford Manor)* above the village.

The war effort eventually wound down in 1946, when the air raid wardens enjoyed a farewell supper in the village hall, while on 27th June, a victory sports day was held on the school field. To commemorate the fallen, the War Memorial was updated and a plaque was put up in the church in 1948. They were dedicated by the Dean of Rochester on 31st July 1949.

Some twenty-one names were added to the twenty already recorded, including that of one woman.

THE POST WAR YEARS

In spite of the continuation of rationing and the shortages of many necessities, the village began to get back to normal as soon as the war was over. Building activity, held up for six years, was resumed at once, and the pile of bricks that had stood at the top of Springhead Road for so long was quickly converted into new houses. Organisations became active, and new ones appeared. Among these was a historical society founded by Mr. C.H. Brett, with Brigadier H.R. Norman as President. In spite of a promising start, this group broke up within years, as members found that their time was fully taken up with more personal and domestic pressures consequent upon the resumption of normal civilian life after the war.

The British Legion branch flourished, as more and more men and women returned from the services. The men met monthly in The Wheatsheaf annexe, and the Women's Section met in the St. Edith Hall. This was the beginning of a long period of social events, such as garden parties, fetes and sports days. The former were held by the Church in the Vicarage garden and at Crowdleham, whilst the British Legion ran fairs in the garden at Wybournes. School sports days brought all the village together year by year. The Cricket Club matches were another attraction and the club was able to lay a new table on the Common Field in 1948 after its restoration to public use.

Mr. Scipio died suddenly in January 1949 about a year after losing his wife. In her memory he had given an electric blower for the Gurn Organ, and in his memory the congregation gave a silver gilt ciborium. His last major work was the re-shingling of the tower and spire of the church. This was done with Canadian red cedar instead of the oak shingles that had been put on seventy years before. The cost of this work and that of a new cross at the top of the spire was partly covered by the expedient of "selling" shingles to the public who for sixpence could write their name on a shingle.

The new Vicar, the Revd. John Aquila Lloyd, was instituted on

31st May 1949 by Dr. Chavasse, Bishop of Rochester. An active business-like man, ably supported by his wife and his twin son and daughter, Mr. Lloyd carried on the good works of his predecessor. He was responsible for introducing the rule that fortunately still obtains in Kemsing, that any meeting advertised to start at a given hour should start promptly at that time. He also formed a branch of the Church of England Men's Society which produced a pool of volunteers for work about the church and churchyard, besides providing a forum for deep discussions, held mostly in the homes of the various members before the advent of a church hall. His eloquent reading of the lessons in church attracted many a visitor from other parishes. More unfortunately, his love of music and insistence on controlling the choice of hymns and anthems to be sung in church, brought him into conflict with more than one organist, until the appointment of Mr. S. R. Smart in 1953. Another of his musical institutions was called "The Kemsingers" - a group of people who met in the Vicarage and gave performances regularly. This group was eventually disbanded. Until this time the parish magazine had been of the old quarto size and Mr. Lloyd had this reduced to octavo, which he thought would be easier to distribute and would meet with the approval of its readers. This change was made in 1950, a year in which many other changes were brought about. The lack of a church hall was becoming more and more apparent, as village activities increased, and meeting places became inadequate. So some ex-army huts were purchased, and erected in the corner of Cleves Orchard, next to the church. This orchard had been planted out in the early 1900s by Mr. Skarratt, and it contained specimens of nearly every kind of fruit to be grown in England, including several apples *(Russet, Wine Sap, Bramley Seedling, Blenheim Orange, Grenadier and Wellington)*. There were pears, greengages, cobnuts, medlars, plums and quince, while peaches and apricots were trained on the red brick wall, built specially for the purpose, which now divides the Youth Hostel grounds from the burial ground. The new "hall" measured about fifteen feet by thirty feet with a small addition at the north end for a tiny kitchen and toilets. It was dedicated and opened on 15th November 1951.

Lord Norman, who had been living at St. Clere since Sir Mark E. Collet left in 1935, died in February 1950, a memorial service being held on the 18th. St. Clere then became the home of Brigadier and Mrs. H.R. Norman, who had been living in Nearly Corner since the end of the war.

Church expenditure was largely caused by theft and dilapidation. In October 1951 eight hundred pounds' worth of lead was stripped from the flat roof of the Vicar's vestry and had to be replaced by copper sheeting, costing a hundred and sixty-five pounds. The south side of the chancel roof, with the north and south sides of the nave roof and of the porch were re-tiled at a cost of £300. The church architects at this time were Messrs. Caroe and Partners, and the firm contracting to do the work was Roberts Adlard & Co. of Rochester.

Some of the cost for making these repairs was covered by the proceeds of an exhibition of church treasures, organised by the Vicar on St. Edith's Day, 16th September 1950, which had formed the basis of a new fabric fund.

Changes in church personnel included the election of Mr. P.E.C. Burrows as churchwarden in place of Mr. J.G. Bevington; the appointment of Mr. Sidney Larcombe as acting organist; and the employment of Mr. W. Hook of Otford as verger. More changes in personnel followed in 1951. In June, Brigadier Lawrence became the church treasurer in place of Mr. L.B. Burtt. Mr. Lowing had resigned as headmaster of the school in September 1950 and was succeeded by Mr. S.R. Smart who was appointed from a shortlist of eight chosen from a hundred and forty-two applicants. He instituted a Parent-Teachers Association from which grew other organisations. These were the drama group, which after combining with the Women's Institute drama group, was the forerunner of the Kemsing Amateur Dramatic Society *(K.A.D.S.)* later re-named the Kemsing Players; and the country dance group which continues to meet weekly.

Another organisation which counts Mr. Smart as a founder-member was the Kemsing Gardeners Society, which was dreamed up during a casual conversation in The Bell between, among others,

Mr. Smart, Mr. C.H. Brett, and Mr. R.B. Bray. A suggestion that such a group should be formed and called the Kemsing Horticultural Association was agreed but modified as to the title which Mr. Smart felt would be more applicable in a village as the Kemsing Gardeners Society. At a meeting in the village hall in 1952 the society was inaugurated with Mr. Smart as chairman, Messrs. Brett and Bray on the committee, and Mr. Brian Jolley as first secretary. This year also saw the formation of The Kemsing Badminton Club.

A new group of residents over sixty years of age was formed at a meeting called by the Women's Institute and held in the old chapel in St. Edith's Road. It was called the Darby and Joan Club, and the first leaders were Mrs. Smart and her mother, Mrs. Rome. The name was changed many years later to the Evergreens.

As more houses were being built in Park Lane and Rushymead and at the council house estate north of Dynes Road, the population recorded by the fifteenth national census of 1951 was up to 2,363 living in 690 houses. This represented over 1,400 more people arriving in the twenty years since the previous census in 1931, and more than three times the number of houses. The Post Office began to experience difficulties in delivering mail, since most houses were known by name only, and they instituted a system of numbering.

The death of King George VI was marked by a memorial service held on 15th February 1952, and the coronation of Queen Elizabeth II on 2nd June 1953 was anticipated by preparations for a carnival and other celebrations. In the event, the weather was inclement, and the carnival procession much reduced in splendour. However, the carnival queen, Miss Gladys Parkin and her attendants, Miss Ann Fisher and Miss Rose Mitchell, rode through the village followed by groups and individuals variously dressed, with floats manned by members of several organisations. The school had changed its status in the September before, and was now a County Primary School for children up to eleven years of age, those over that age having been transferred to County Secondary Schools, so the younger school children were entertained at the school. Outdoor fun was precluded by the weather but a good tea was enjoyed and each child received a coronation mug. In the evening a bonfire was lit on Green Hill. One effect of the coronation celebrations throughout the country was the increased popularity of television sets. Many people had viewed the coronation service in Westminster Abbey while crowded into the sitting rooms of their more fortunate neighbours. Mr and Mrs. V. Robbins had opened a television hire shop in the West End in 1952 and by 1954 they had prospered enough to be able to move their business into Sevenoaks town.

The mission room, known to local people in Noah's Ark as the "Tin Hut", was deemed no longer necessary by the Parochial Church Council, and negotiations resulted in its sale. The money received, some two hundred and forty pounds, was set aside towards a fund for providing a new church hall.

Changes in the village scene involved the building of Collet Road, Barnfield Crescent, Northdown Road and Hillside Road by the Sevenoaks Rural District Council, and of the first bungalows in Highfield Road by the Westminster Self-Build Association. At the same time, the West End, which until then had not included Rossiters Hill, which was merely a cart track, was widened all the way to its junction with Childsbridge Lane.

Mr. Smart at the old Gern organ. The ladder led to the rood screen loft.

Also in 1953, Mr. Smart was appointed church organist when Mr. Sydney Larcombe resigned. As headmaster of the school, Mr. Smart was in a good position to select boys with promising voices, and by 1954, there was a very good church choir of men and boys. For many years from 1928 to 1953, Mr. Jack Burt was sexton/verger. The post of sexton was then dropped, while that of verger passed from Mr. William Hook who died suddenly in June 1953, to Mr. Eric Bangay who resigned soon after; and then to Mr. Alfred Haynes who held the job for nearly thirty years. Since his retirement in 1981 there has been no verger. On the civic side, Mr. Joseph Brewer, clerk to the Parish Council for four years, retired and Mrs. E. Cornford, secretary to Brigadier Norman at St. Clere, was appointed. The status of Kemsing as a small village was somewhat altered when the telephone exchange at Seal, to which Kemsing exchange had been transferred, was itself closed, and Kemsing people found that they had either Sevenoaks or Otford numbers.

Mr. Lloyd's final two years as Vicar before leaving for the benefice of Leybourne, were filled with activity in church life, and throughout the parish. The old organ had to be extensively repaired, and a plaque to Lord Norman was installed in the north aisle. An inspection by experts was made of the remaining vestiges of wall paintings. They were deemed to be too far deteriorated for recovery, but some of the original eleven consecration crosses were worth marking. These have, in fact, all disappeared in turn. Mr. G. Gilbert, an assistant organist, presented a new credence table, made by himself, together with a pair of oak flower stands for the sanctuary.

Rochester Diocese celebrated its jubilee of one thousand four hundred years with an exhibition in the cathedral where Kemsing's Elizabethan chalice was on display. The jubilee offering made by St. Mary's took the form of a cheque for fifty pounds which was presented to the new church of St. Barnabas, St. Mary Cray. Members of the choir and congregation also made a pilgrimage to Otford church along the Pilgrims Way.

Building continued throughout the parish. The Highfield Road development was the location for a United Nations Association working camp, attended by overseas students. There were about fifty in all at any one time during the summer of 1955. They worked on the buildings and also performed charitable works in the Sevenoaks area. Kemsing gave them a good welcome, and entertained them in their leisure hours. At a final party held in the old church hall, boys and girls of a dozen nationalities were the guests of the church congregation.

Another building project in 1956 was the demolition of the old St. Edith Farmhouse and its rebuilding by Mr. Jack Parkin, who found while work was progressing, that the original house had been built in 1655 and rebuilt in 1772. Meanwhile, Orchard Way houses and bungalows were being occupied by their first residents.

The Darby and Joan Club was in the hands of a new leader, Mrs. K. Lowing, wife of the former headmaster, who founded a separate group called the Over Sixties Choir, with her husband as conductor and herself as pianist. The chairmanship of the Parish Council also changed hands in 1955 when Mr. Henry Henry took over from Mr. Gershom Williams, who had been in office for some nineteen years.

The voluntary library, housed in the club room at the back of The Bell Inn, was taken over by Mrs. Berry and Mrs. Fielden in 1954 from Mr Brian Jolley and Mrs. Cook, who had succeeded Miss Waddilove, one of the teachers at the school. There were some three hundred books on loan to about fifty regular borrowers.

ST. EDITH'S FARMHOUSE

Chapter 14
1956 To 1976

The Revd. G.M. Young

Mr. C.J. Pinney, the people's churchwarden, retired early in 1956, and Mr. V.E. Bowden, who had been secretary to the PCC since 1946, was elected in his place. There was an interregnum of some months after Mr. Lloyd left Kemsing in the autumn of 1956 to be inducted as Rector of Leybourne. His successor was the Revd. G.M. Young, Vicar of Farningham, who was instituted to the living of Kemsing in February 1957.

During the interregnum, Mr. P.E.C. Burrows, the Vicar's warden, supervised repairs which had to be made to the north side of the nave and chancel roofs, and a certain amount of damage from dry rot in the church had to be dealt with. The latter cost fifty-five pounds, but much more serious damage by death watch beetle cost five hundred and fifty-four pounds the following year.

Mr. Smart revived the scout group towards the end of 1956 with himself as group scoutmaster, and Mrs. West and Mrs. Payne as cub masters. April 1958 saw the founding of the Evening W.I.

More house building further increased the population. Wulfred Way was completed and the Springhead Estate (*Castle Drive*,

Montfort Road, Boleyn Road, Edgar Road, and Nightingale Road) was started. Some of the new residents quickly raised the question of street lighting, but voting went against it.

The St. Edith Hall had been showing signs of wear for the past year or so, and a group of volunteers formed themselves into an association called the Friends of the St. Edith Hall under the chairmanship of Mr. A.P. Hunt with Mr. J.E.T. Horne as treasurer. Their express purpose was to raise enough money to have the hall re-wired. As soon as this was completed in February 1958 at a cost of a hundred pounds, the group was disbanded. Inside the hall a new piece of furniture appeared in 1957 in the shape of a chairman's table and chair, which was presented by his family and friends in memory of the late Mr. Guido Sting, former chairman of the hall management committee.

Mr Young organised a gift day and ran an exhibition of church treasures in the church in July 1958. The Grundy furnace was in need of repair which was estimated to cost three hundred and seventy-one pounds, so a "371 committee" was formed, and the members raised the money by a house to house collection.

In recent years the church income had been supported by an envelope system, but in 1959 Mr. Young suggested to the PCC that they should study the new American approach to fundraising, which was known as the Wells System. At first, this way of approaching the problem was not viewed with favour in many English parishes, but where it was adopted there was no doubt of its success. After two years of study and discussion, it was agreed to go for this Christian Stewardship, and plans were made for a campaign to take place in 1961. Under the guidance of Mr. *(later Sir)* John Best-Shaw, several "visitors" were commissioned at a special service, and during the next few days made their way round the parish explaining the system. A supper party was held to which parishioners were invited, and at which the principles of stewardship were set out by a few speakers who had been groomed for the task. An office was set up at No. 1 The Landway, where Mr. Best-Shaw and his secretary gathered and collated the results of the visitors' efforts. Thus, by October 1961, Christian Stewardship was well established at St. Mary's.

The Noah's Ark mission room had been sold with a view to providing enough money to build a larger church hall. This project ran all through the summer of 1961 under the aegis of a committee chaired by Mr. V.E. Bowden with Mr. S.R. Smart as secretary. The old army huts were demolished, a new and larger base laid, and a professional company engaged to raise the walls and fit the roof. After that all the finishing work was done by voluntary labour. This entailed constructing an approach and steps to the door, and a cement path all the way round; plumbing; and wiring for electricity. Both interior and exterior were decorated by volunteers, much of the painting inside being done well on into October and November in the evenings.

THE MILLENNIUM OF ST. EDITH

This busy year saw the first St. Edith Festival. It was realised that as St. Edith had been born in Kemsing in AD 961, 1961 would see the millennium of her birth. The suggestion made at a PCC meeting in 1960 by the People's warden, Mr. Bowden, that this should be marked in some way, was taken up by Mr. Young, the Vicar. He was a parish councillor, and he put it to the Parish Council that the whole village should be included in this project. Thereupon, a small committee was formed led by Mrs. Doris Dew. Celebrations were planned for the week commencing 10th September, culminating in a special service on the 17th, which was the day after St. Edith's Feast day, when the new Bishop of Rochester, Dr. David Say, came to the village for the first of his many visits. He dedicated a stone plaque placed in the wall of the well area. For this ceremony, the old tradition of processing to St. Edith's well on her feast day was revived, and the banner which had been made specially for the event in 1926 was once more carried in procession from the church to the well, a custom which has persisted ever since. The previous week saw meetings of every kind involving every organisation in the parish. They included choir concerts; the production of a play called "Echoes from the Well", specially written for the occasion by Leslie Cormack; an exhibition of church treasures and a talk on the history of the church; a supper dance; a talk on Old Kemsing illustrated by slides; a country dance party; and bingo and whist drives. A carnival procession through the village on the Saturday featured many decorated floats, including one bearing the Festival Queen, Jaqueline Wills, and her attendants, Shirley Hodges and Sylvia Glover, and led to displays and entertainments on the Common Field. The week closed with Evensong and a procession in church, the speaker being the Revd. Canon R.V. Bristow, former vicar of the parish. Many of the above listed events were held in the St. Edith Hall, which was that year celebrating its golden jubilee.

The sixteenth national census 1961 revealed that the population of Kemsing had risen to 3,907 living in 1,183 houses, 493 houses having been built in the previous decade. Cleves Road was completed. A further sixteen bungalows were built the following year in Church Lane, designed to house senior citizens. To enable this development to be made, special steps had to be taken to overcome the covenant governing the use of the Common Field. It was in 1961 that Lady Lyle, the widow of Sir Oliver Lyle, sold Shorehill and its grounds to the Hildenborough Hall Evangelical Trust, who re-named the house Hildenborough Hall.

On January 21st 1962 Mr. Young baptised Rebecca Lucy Stephens, little knowing that she was to become the first British woman to climb Mount Everest.

In 1963 the Parish Council and the Parochial Church Council finally came to an agreement about the provision and maintenance of a new burial ground, thus completing negotiations which had been going on since 1951 when it had been forecast that the churchyard would soon be full. Under this agreement, which was to last until 1993, the Church divided Cleves Orchard which was in their possession into two parts, the northern part to be a burial ground and the southern part, which included the church hall, to be a recreation field for youth activities. All the mature fruit trees in the orchard were bulldozed and burnt and a beech hedge was planted to divide the two areas. On 21st June 1963, Bishop Mann,

Assistant Bishop of Rochester, consecrated the new burial ground. Management of both the old churchyard and the new area was vested in a committee made up of members of both the Parish Council and the Parochial Church Council.

The Parish Council at this time was enlarged from nine to eleven members, and Mrs. Doris Dew succeeded Mr. Henry Henry, who had been chairman since 1955.

The number of school children was still on the increase and the third stage of the enlargement of the school, another classroom, was completed. Other building operations included a cul-de-sac on the site of a bungalow called "Greystones" in Childsbridge Lane. The first name suggested for this development was Hunsdon Road after an Elizabethan Lord of the Manor. This was not accepted, and the name Sidley Road was adopted, commemorating former owners of St. Clere. This name was disliked by the new residents, who successfully appealed for it to be changed to Greystones Close.

Dr John Robinson began the building of a house and surgery in West End at the close of 1963, and with a view to further housing needs, the Vicar, Mr. Young, arranged for the sale of the northern part of the Vicarage garden to the Sevenoaks Rural District Council for the future building of old people's bungalows. These were not, in fact, built until 1973, and contrary to the wishes of the Parochial Church Council in 1963, only two bungalows were built, the rest of the development consisting of a two-storey block with two flats and a house for the warden.

In the year 1964, very severe weather was the keynote. Snow had started to fall on the previous Boxing Day and was still on the ground together with further falls the following March. For some days the village was cut off.

Building work continued into 1964, when alterations were made to the interior of the St. Edith Hall - the door in the foyer leading to the men's toilet being moved and a new entrance to it made in the west wall of the hall. The hall and stage were all redecorated. On 16th September, a plaque, set under the statue of St. Edith outside the hall, was dedicated, after a civic service in church followed by a procession to the hall. The inscription on the stone commemorated the gift of the hall to the village by Sir Mark E. Collet in 1911. Those present included Brigadier Norman and members of his family, Canon R.V. Bristow, and the Revd. G.M. Young.

As for houses, new developments were being made at West End, where an estate of Scandinavian type houses were erected by Mr. Peploe of Shoreham in the grounds of a house called "Copperfield". The house was later demolished to make room for Copperfields Close, whilst Copperfields Orchard was built in part of the garden of the house called "Peveril". Some years later Copperfields Walk was built in the gardens of some houses in Childsbridge Lane.

On the cultural side, the Kemsing Singers was formed by Mr. Thomas Denyer, and Mr. F. Hooper. In August an exhibition of pictures by local artists was held in the church hall.

The postmistress, Mrs. Forbes, decided to leave the village, thus breaking a link between the Post Office and the Holden family lasting almost a hundred years. After Andrew Holden's death, his daughter, Mrs. Walker, had carried on, followed by a relative, Mr. Archibald Fiveash, who moved the Post Office from Clement House to No. 1 St. Edith's Road, and then Mrs. Forbes, who was another family connection. The new owners of the Post Office were Mr and Mrs Ellis, who had the newsagents shop in Dynes Road.

The main events of the year 1965 concerned the church, as Mr. Young instituted a major restoration of the interior. The old Gern organ was dismantled, and its various parts sold to interested parties, including Sevenoaks School, where some of the pipes were incorporated into an organ that they were building. This meant that the arch between the north aisle and the vestry was revealed, and the woodcarvings that had held the pipes in place were discarded. A spiral stair was erected in the vestry to give access to the loft on which a Miller electronic organ was installed. *(The latter proved unsatisfactory after some years, and was replaced in 1973 by a new pipe organ, built by Ralph Arnold of Orpington. The pipes were concealed by laying them horizontally on the rood screen loft).*

Meanwhile the walls of the nave were whitened and the prayer boards repainted and put up on the south wall, replacing two large oil paintings which had hung there for many years. The 1721 Royal Coat of Arms was moved from the south to the north wall of the aisle, after restoration by Mr. C.H. Brett and Mr. R.A. Edwards.

Mr. E.G. Cowlard, who had been churchwarden for the past year, resigned and Mr. Douglas Woodcock was elected to fill his place. In December, the Vicar of Kemsing, the Revd. G.M. Young was made Priest-in-Charge of St. Mary's Church, Woodlands. Running two parishes meant calling upon more help from the lay readers, Mr. E.G. Cowlard and Mr. Robin Long, in order to be able to hold services on Sundays in both churches.

More houses were built on land in West End after the demolition in January 1965 of the house called Dippers Hall. This house, built at the end of the 19th century and then called South View, was renamed Dippers Hall at some time later, after a house which had stood there or thereabouts for some three hundred years. The new development, consisting of thirty-one houses, was called Dippers Close.

A sample census taken in 1966, indicated that some hundred and seventeen houses had been built in the previous five years.

At about this time Mrs. Lowing relinquished the leadership of the Darby and Joan Club to Miss Eva Smith; and another stalwart, Mrs. Hurren, retired after twenty-four years as caretaker of the St. Edith Hall.

A Church Week was held from 26th June 1966. Events included a choir recital and a musical performance; country dancing; a play by the Kemsing Amateur Dramatic Society; a concert by the Kemsing Singers; a flower festival and exhibition of church treasures. The week was brought to a close by the singing of a solemn Te Deum at Evensong on 3rd July.

In his last year as Vicar of Kemsing, Mr. Young changed the format of the parish magazine again. The small monthly edition introduced by Mr. Lloyd had been replaced in 1960 by a quarto-sized monthly. In consultation with Mr. B.J. Burt, who acted as printing adviser to many organisations in the village, he introduced a quarterly magazine in a smaller size. He called it "The Well" after St. Edith's well, because that had been a meeting place and centre for discussion about village affairs for centuries.

CANON JOHN

Mr. Young moved away to be the Vicar of West Malling at the end of 1966 and the Revd. J.H. Rahe Hughes was instituted as Vicar of Kemsing and Priest-in-Charge of St. Mary's Woodlands on 3rd February 1967. He was a bachelor and brought his mother to stay at the vicarage with him. He had been the Vicar of an Orpington parish, where he was currently organising a pilgrimage walk to Canterbury. Wishing to remain connected with this project, he involved a number of his new parishioners in the venture, some of them acting as stewards and others joining the walkers. The Vicar himself completed the walk, albeit with some difficulty. He became very popular in the village, and after having been made Rural Dean of Shoreham in January 1968, he was known to all in the parish as "Canon John". His incumbency of nine years was a period of great activity and development in all aspects of village life.

The church held two Christian Stewardship campaigns, in 1969 and 1972. Canon John held open house at the Vicarage, a fact that was much appreciated by many a youth hosteller, who had arrived too late to get into the hostel.

Fresh gifts to the church included an altar cloth, dedicated on 8th November 1970, and intended for use on Remembrance Sundays in future years; a wrought iron candlestick, given by Miss M.A. Hudson in memory of her mother; a festival altar frontal in white with the MR monogram, given by the Pilgrims Working Party, who, under the leadership of Mrs. Katherine Ford, went on to provide the church with new kneelers and also paid for a new church noticeboard, carved in oak by Mr. George Chapman in 1975. Oak shelves were fitted to the two two-light windows in the north aisle, to facilitate flower decorating for festivals, and an oak drop table was fitted behind the pew next to the font. On Ash Wednesday 1974 a new Lenten altar frontal, dossal, and side curtains were used for the first time. They were presented anonymously and designed and worked in Spanish black work by two parishioners. The remaining parts of this Lenten array, a chasuble and stole, maniple, veil and burse, pulpit fall, and book marks, were added the following year.

The choir were invited to sing Evensong in the Chapel of St. Peter ad Vincula in the Tower of London in July 1971.

The churchwardens at this time were Mr. S.J. Payne, who had succeeded Mr. D.W. Woodcock, and Mr. Tom Dew. One less favourable feature at this time was the demise of the Kemsing branch of the Church of England Men's Society, after a period of several years. Members of the branch had been responsible for introducing an annual overseas weekend for students from all over the world. These young people were accommodated in houses around the village, worshipped at the morning service, were entertained in the church hall afterwards, and were given a general tour of the village.

Canon Rahe Hughes, until then Priest-in-Charge of St. Mary's, Woodlands, was made Vicar of that parish by an Order in Council of 14th May 1975, a few days before his retirement.

In 1972, the Parish Council increased in size from eleven to thirteen members with Mr. D.A. Eley as Chairman, in succession to Mr. W. Roxburgh, who had served for just one year. In September 1967 application was made for the building of a scout hut and youth club on land in the West End, opposite Dippers Close. This was not approved, and subsequently permission was granted in April 1972 for the building of a scout hut on the Common Field. This was successfully carried out, largely by voluntary labour.

Several parish walks were organised to places of local interest, such as Yaldham Manor, Stonepitts, St. Clere, West Kingsdown Mill and Otford. These were always well supported. In 1974, a guide to the Kemsing footpaths was published by the Parish Council.

Numbers of children attending the school were still increasing and in March 1967 two new classrooms were erected, followed in June that year by the roofing over of the swimming pool, which had been provided by the Parent Teacher Association. In May 1971, the school house was extended to accommodate the family of the new headmaster, Mr. Allan Gilbert, who had succeeded Mr. S.R. Smart on the retirement of the latter in July 1969.

Several new groups and organisations came into being between 1960 and 1980. In September 1967 an Arts Club was formed, meeting weekly in the St. Edith Hall. This was initially very popular but unfortunately collapsed within a few years. The Gardening Society went from strength to strength and on 20th February 1970 were the hosts to the radio programme "Gardeners Question Time". An offshoot of the Gardeners Society was the Wildflower Group which first met in September 1970. This is an informal gathering without any sort of constitution, but still attracts enthusiasts. In that same month, September 1970, the Kemsing Society was formed. This was in spite of the fact that when it had been suggested some months before that Kemsing should, like other villages in the district, have such a society to keep an eye on progress of events, buildings, etc. in the village, the chairman of the Parish

Council at that time convinced the meeting that all such work was amply covered by the Parish Council and there was no need for a separate society. The Society's most notable achievement was the organising of a petition, which was eventually successful, to have the northern half of the Common Field restored to public use and to have it laid out to grass and planted with trees. The chairman of the Society, which ceased to exist after a few years, was Mr. F. Lacey. He died very soon afterwards and in his memory a seat was erected on the Common Field.

A sports club was formed in 1971, called the Pilgrim Sports Club, followed in November 1973 by the founding of the Kemsing Sports Association, which was very soon joined by a great number of families.

Considerable building activity took place, including an extension to the Working Men's Club to the plan left for this purpose by Sir Mark Collet. It was opened in November 1969 by Brigadier Norman. Another opening of a public building took place in January 1970, when Mr. Colin Cowdrey performed this function at the newly built library on the corner of Dippers Close.

In preparation for the Kemsing Festival of 1971, the Working Men's Club had removed the grass banks that were in front of the St. Edith Hall. This second St. Edith Festival was held in September and lasted for two weeks. Mrs D.I. Dew was Chairman of the organising committee with Mr. V.E. Bowden as secretary. The Festival Queen, who with her attendants Geraldine Tonkin and Doreen Lloyd attended nearly every function, was Penny Covington.

At about this time also, Mr. John Bradley secured and erected outside his house "Little Wybournes" a large ornamental clock. This was kept in going order until some years later, when the barn to which it was attached became a 'granny flat' and the working of the clock was too noisy for comfort. Seats were provided in various spots on Green Hill above the village. At Heverham, Mr. John Burrluck, the publican at The Chequers opened a restaurant in the barn next door. Also in 1971, the proprietors of Hildenborough Hall extended the building southwards and installed a swimming pool. It was at this time that the lychgate and the west gate of the churchyard were provided with new gates. The coffin post which used to stand in the middle of the large lychgate was discarded.

Housing was on the increase, and in 1972 work began on the building of the council flats in Park Lane, while in December 1972 Chart View was nearly finished and Mary Burrows Gardens was begun. This development was named to commemorate the devoted work for the village over a period of forty years of Miss Mary Burrows, MBE, Alderman of Kent. It was opened by her brother, Sir John Burrows, on 26th November, 1973.

The year 1973 was "Plant a Tree in Seventy-three" year, and a committee was formed to organise the planting of several hundred trees throughout the parish. Some of these did not survive, but a great number of trees now furnishing the village were planted at that time, including the large wood which occupies the north-east corner of the Common Field.

In the village itself, a much patronised and appreciated grocer's shop at Yew Tree House was closed and the house returned to private use.

Kemsing Branch Library

Chapter 15
Bringing The Story Up To Date

Mr And Mrs Daniels

From 1975 to 1982 the Revd. K.P.T. Daniels was Vicar of Kemsing and Woodlands. With the support of his wife, Betty, and daughter, Catherine, he gave a great lead to the social life of the parish and was a much respected spiritual adviser. He was inducted to the living on 17th July 1975. During his incumbency several repairs were made to the church. In 1978, the south-west buttress had to be strengthened and made to support the west wall from which it had been gradually falling away. Two of the windows in the north aisle were repaired, and the west door was overhauled and put into good condition by Mr. Kenneth Saunders. Four years later, in June 1982, the west wall was stripped of its remaining medieval plaster. This was after much consultation with the church architect, who was reluctant to lose the plaster, but who was eventually pleased with the result, for it revealed the fact that the west wall had been built in an entirely different style from the rest of the church. Why this should be so has not yet been explained.

In 1975, the Parish Council had to deal with a new problem that has beset many a parish in the country. A firm called Yalepalm Ltd. of Bradwell-on-Sea, Essex, acquired twenty-one acres of land north of the Pilgrims Way, between The Landway and Childsbridge Lane, and sold it off in some two hundred and seventy-seven plots, designated "leisure plots". Such development has caused considerable trouble in some places, and Kemsing Parish Council took steps immediately to ensure that no such trouble would be experienced here. The land is still owned by several different people, but has not been spoiled in any way; in fact it has become a very interesting unofficial wildflower reserve. In 1975 also the Parish Council appointed a small committee to make and publish an appraisal of the village on lines set out by the Kent Council of Social Service, and they also produced a guide to the listed buildings in the parish, of which there are no less than twenty-seven. This was followed in July 1980 by the publication of the Kemsing Down Nature Reserve guide.

At the west end of the village, an old people's home called "The Dynes" was opened on 30th January 1976 by Mr. John White, the chairman of the Kent County Council.

Behind The Wheatsheaf, a car park was laid out in conjunction with Sevenoaks District Council in January 1978, and paving stones were laid outside the Village Hall. Because the St. Edith Hall was so well booked throughout the year, steps had to be taken to increase accommodation, and the Small Hall was built, to include a new kitchen, green room and toilets. These additional facilities were opened in 1979 by Mr. Ronnie Norman.

Another move by the Parish Council was the formation in 1976 of an Allotment Holders Association on land leased from Kent Education Committee, and on land in Noah's Ark given to the Parish Council by Mr. Ian Pattullo. Mr. Brian Buttifant was the first chairman of the association. A further purchase made by the Parish Council this year was an area of land on the downs above the village which included Whiteleaf Down, Shorehill Down and Shorehill Wood. These now form part of the Kemsing Down Nature Reserve.

Two new organisations appeared in 1975 and 1976. The first was called the Shorehill Music Society, into which was incorporated the Kemsing Singers, and the second was the Kemsing

Evening Forum which was founded by Mrs. B. Goldsmith, Mrs. J. Harrison, and Mrs. J. Wilkinson, for ladies who lived mostly in the west end of the village and were not members of other women's organisations. The scouts celebrated the fiftieth anniversary of scouting in Kemsing on 26th June 1976. 1977 was the year of Queen Elizabeth's Jubilee and to mark this celebrations were held in the month of June. An exhibition of royal pictures and artefacts was held in the Box House; there was dancing in the High Street in the evening; and a bonfire was lit on Green Hill. This was attended by a procession of people who had been to Hildenborough Hall for an alfresco concert and who marched down the footpath to the bonfire carrying lighted torches. At the end of the evening, a salvo of twenty-five rockets was fired, each one counted down very loudly by the onlookers. A tree planted on the Common Field, and a rose bed set out on the green in Dynes Road also commemorated the Jubilee.

In September 1977, Park Lane was widened and a barn which had stood on the St. Edith's Road corner was demolished. This gave better access to the new council houses and flats which had been built in Park Lane. A year or two later Norman Close at the far end of Nightingale Road was planned, and finally occupied. At Heverham changes took the form of the conversion of some farm buildings at Manor House Farm into three dwellings in the year 1980. In May that year a village sign was erected on the green next to St. Edith's well, close to the village butcher's shop. The latter had been shut for several months since the death of the last of the Wellbeloved family to own it, but re-opened on 20th October 1980, under the management of Mr. David Garrett. A great change in the background to the village was marked by the opening of the M.26 Motorway by Mr. Norman Fowler on 18th November 1980. Two years later, in May 1982, gas was carried along the Pilgrims Way and down Childsbridge Lane and The Landway.

1981 was the year of the third Kemsing Festival, which ran from 6th to 20th September, and was organised by a committee chaired by Mr. Sydney Swann with Miss Doreen Roberts as secretary. Again, a full two weeks of exhibitions, and similar events was supported by every organisation in the village. The Festival Queen was Caroline Bryans and she was attended by Ann Richardson and Tracy Stachini.

RICHARD THE TENTH

On the retirement of Mr. Daniels the Revd. Richard W. Bateman was instituted to the vicarage on 7th January 1983. He became the seventy-third known incumbent of the parish, and the tenth to have the name Richard. He was also the first to become known to most of his congregation by his Christian name. His ministry was noted for innovations, both in church worship and in church administration and maintenance. The Alternative Services Book was introduced and emphasis was laid on the importance of family worship and the encouragement of young parents to participate in the conduct of the services. Pastoral Assistants were appointed and lay people were licensed to administer the chalice. More and more women joined the list of readers of the lessons, and contributed in many other ways towards the celebration of the Eucharist and the conduct of church services in general.

Mr. Bateman soon set about making some improvements to the church building. In April 1983, he had the nave and north aisle redecorated and the footplates of the lychgate repaired. At the same time, an iron grille was inserted into the roof of the lychgate to deter vandals from removing the tiles. When all this was completed, he installed a burglar alarm system to ensure that the body of the church could be kept open every day throughout daylight hours. Weekly lunches provided in the church hall meant that the kitchen and its equipment had to be brought up to the requirements of Age Concern, the organisers of these lunches, which were staffed by volunteers. Heating in the church involved discarding the old Grundy hot air system and installing electrically controlled radiators. To finance this in part an exhibition was held in 1985 of vestments and flower arrangements. In June 1990, Mr. Bateman organised a Festival of Creation and Creativity involving all organisations in the parish. Good weather conditions prevailed and the whole week's events were successfully carried out. In the following year, Mr. Bateman and the Revd. Paul Cox, Headmaster of St. Michael's School, Otford, left the district together to take over the welfare of eight small parishes in the Canterbury area.

It had been one of Mr. Bateman's plans to remove the pews from under the tower and to make that area a welcoming feature for newcomers and visitors. This scheme was opposed at a meeting held in the church and the Vicar agreed not to proceed. However, after his departure and before a new vicar had been instituted, the Parochial Church Council arranged for the pews to be removed and put into storage in case they were required again later. This did not arise, as a gift of a new peal of bells and the formation of the team of bell ringers who needed the space in which to operate, rendered their restoration undesirable. The pews were eventually sold to parishioners.

In the 1980s the Parish Council had to deal with copious applications for planning permission. The opening of the Chaucer

Business Park in 1985 in Watery Lane was only the beginning of a series of requests as the facilities there were increased year by year, and the approach from the A25 had to be improved by lowering the level of the road under the railway bridge.

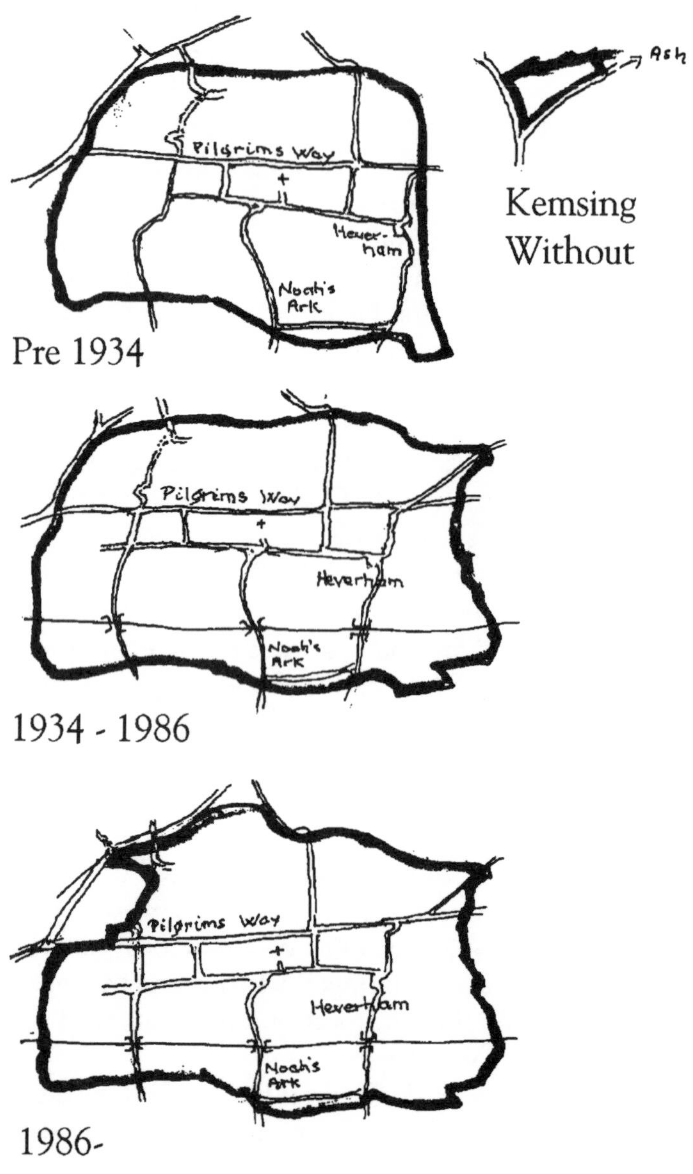

The parish boundaries made in 1934 remained in force until 1986, when St. Michael's School and its grounds were taken into Otford parish, and a similar area of Shoreham parish between Birchin Cross Road and Cotmans Ash Road was added to Kemsing parish.

Other building operations during the 1980s included the demolition of all the Airey houses in the parish, and the provision of new council houses in their place. This operation was carried out by the Sevenoaks District Council in just a few months in 1985. Another small development was made off the West End by the erection of the eight houses in Copperfields Walk, mentioned earlier.

Airey Houses

A Youth Club founded by the Parish Council in January 1984 had a chequered career but has continued to operate ever since.

In July 1988 a Beacon Fire was lit on the top of Green Hill to commemorate the approach of the Spanish Armada in the year 1588. The Parish Council were very grateful to the manager and staff of Otford Manor *(formerly Hildenborough Hall)* for the help they provided for this occasion.

As ever, new groups and organisations were forming in this decade. These included the founding in November 1982 of the Wildlife Group sponsored by Mr. Clifford Steel. Monthly meetings were held in the small St. Edith Hall attended by a sizeable group of regular supporters.

A Kemsing Squash Club formed in January 1984 met at first at St. Clere, but was able to move into the new Sir Mark Collet Pavilion on the Common Field in 1987, when the Kemsing Sports Association saw the opening of the Pavilion by Mr. Ronnie Norman as the fruition of their endeavours over a number of years. The running of the Pavilion was then entrusted to members of a Pavilion Management Committee under the auspices of five trustees, Mr. Allen Bryant being appointed as the first Manager.

November 18th 1986 saw the inaugural meeting of a new society called the Kemsing Historical & Art Society. The meeting was convened by four residents who felt that there was a need for such a society in the village, which feeling was confirmed by the immediate membership of over two hundred people. The society aimed to meet monthly, to enjoy talks on history, including local history, and art subjects, arranged to be acceptable to all shades of interest. The first chairman, Mr. Walter Williamson, was succeeded in 1989 by Mrs. Melinda Robinson.

Two 75th anniversaries were celebrated in 1986 - the St. Edith Hall Management Committee marked the anniversary of the building of the hall by holding a party at which a specially engraved clock was mounted on the wall next to the stage. This year also saw the 75th anniversary of the founding of the Working Men's Club who held a party in November to mark the occasion. Another 75th anniversary fell in 1990, when the Afternoon Women's Institute put on a party in the village hall and entertained their guests with a tableau of the founding of the branch at the Vicarage *(now Cleves)* in November 1915.

Events of more general concern in this period included the introduction of the one pound coin throughout the country in 1983. There were also great changes of the tree population in the area, caused by the so-called Dutch Elm Disease which removed every large elm tree in the parish, and then on 16th October 1987, by the great hurricane which ravaged so much of south-east England. An extensive planting of trees on Green Hill and in the Nature Reserve met with little initial success owing to the unforeseen sequence of four years of drought. The stream in the well area dried up in 1988, reappeared in 1992,when sufficient rain had fallen to raise the water table high enough to restore the flow and dried up again in 1993.

On 5th February 1991, the Revd. Colin Clive Horn was instituted as Vicar of Kemsing and Woodlands. He and his wife Jan, found themselves immediately involved in preparations for the fourth Kemsing Festival which was due to be held in the September following. The two weeks of events covering all aspects of village life and participated in by all organisations and groups included two dedication services in the church. The first was of the embroidery mounted on the south wall. This had been prepared over a period of two years by a group of forty-five parishioners working under the leadership of Mrs. Margaret Goulding, to record aspects of the village as it was in 1991. The second ceremony took place on the last day of the festival when Bishop J.W. Flagg consecrated the new peal of bells. These had been achieved by melting down two of the existing bells and re-casting them as six smaller ones. The oldest bell was left in situ.

The chairman of the organising committee for the festival was Mr. Ray Ellis, but as he was prevented for personal reasons from attending many of the committee's meetings most of the organising was carried out by Mr. Godfrey Croughton and Mr. Monty Parkin, with Mrs. Jean Cunnew as secretary and Mrs. Margaret Saunders as treasurer.

Before closing this account, it might be of interest to consider how greatly the village and life in it has altered in the last half-century. Changes have been seen to have occurred all down the years but never so markedly as in this last phase. The obvious differences are in the number of houses and therefore of the increase in the population. These are followed by the increased traffic engendered by the easy availability of the motor car. This, in turn, caused the virtual "littering" of the village roads by parked cars belonging to residents whose pre-car era houses had no garages or room for parking. The double gate that closed off the drive of nearly every house in the 1950s has been almost universally abandoned to make it easier to drive off the road. The increase in the number of cars has affected public transport. In 1929 the Women's Institute agitated for public lavatories "as we are now on a bus route". *(Nothing happened about this until 1993!)*. The earliest buses were single deckers operated by private firms. For decades single and double deckers ran to and from Sevenoaks, either via Otford *(London Transport)* or Noah's Ark and Seal *(Maidstone and District)*, Heverham was also catered for, and prior to the widening of West End in 1953 buses had to negotiate the narrowness of The Landway and the Pilgrims Way. In more recent years the lack of support by the public has resulted in a great reduction in services.

Changes in the tree population have been mentioned but another related difference can be seen in the removal of hedges, not only between the cultivated fields but also outside houses where very often walls have taken their place. At night time, although requests to install street lighting have repeatedly been opposed, it is no longer possible to see the stars so well as before, since the lighting on the motorways at Polhill, Wrotham and more distantly, Orpington, reflect into the skies all round Kemsing, so that young children who have never seen the Milky Way confuse that miracle of wonder with a popular sweet bar.

Events and changes constantly follow one another. In 1993 Fairfield Road and Theobalds Close were fully occupied; Dynes Farmhouse was restored, the barn converted and a new group of houses built around them; the old school building was leased by the Parish Council as an extra venue for village and other activities; Rebecca Stephens conquered Mount Everest and Dave Wellman made more adventurous bicycle rides in aid of charities; and Kemsing was judged to be the best kept village in Kent.

More changes will come, but for the time being the story of Kemsing must be brought to a close.

V.E. Bowden
Sandals,
Kemsing

October 1993

KEMSING
KENT
CANTERBURY
PILGRIMS WAY

Index of Appendices

APPENDIX I - RECTORS & VICARS

RECTORS

1265 Richard de Kemsing
1295 Jacobus Sinobaldi
1316 John de Dittone
1326 Richard de Theukesbury
Richard Duraunt
1338 Gilbert de Kekeshill
1341 Thomas de Hope
1347 William de Penbrugge
1353 John de Shippedham
1370 Richard Mowys/Thomas Perd
1383 Richard Heneketon
alias Launston
1396 Thomas Ridlyngton
1399 Adam of Usk

VICARS

1402 Rodelandus Kerbroke
1417 John Jordan/William Mathew
1422 Thomas Stowr
1426 Stephen Porcher
William Aldeborough
1433 Thomas Well
1437 Richard Litelman
1438 John Gorsich
1445 Henry Esthaw
1456 John Willaston
1458 Richard Cutler
1460 William English
1463 Richard Cutler
1477 Robert Snowe
1479 Thomas Marche
1492 William Yanson
1508 William Lincoln
1509 Nicholas Metecalf
1517 Richard Sharpe
1524 Thomas Thebold
1542 John Sennocke
1545 John Denman
1550 Thomas Hicklyng
1554 Thomas Tayllour
1558 Thomas Dale
1561 Gilbert Gennyns
1602 Richard Buckley
1608 Robert Baker
1644 John Baker
1650 Master Marten
1650 Master Bartton
1654 John Stevens
1668 Thomas Stevens
1669 John Tattersall
1674 Maximilian Buck
1720 Robert Parran
1739 Thomas Curteis
1744 Gregory Sharpe
1761 Carswell Winder
1770 William Humphry
1816 Gervas Whitehead
1838 John Netherton Harwood
1846 Thomas O.Blackall
1875 George Bridges Lewis
1889 The Hon. E.V.R. Powys
1889 Thomas Carleton Skarratt
1909 Edward H. Stewart
1924 Ronald Victor Bristow
1931 Harold T. Graham
1934 Charles H.E. Freeman
1936 Vincent Macreth
1939 Albert Edward Scipio
1949 John Aquila Lloyd
1957 Geoffrey Maxwell Young
1967 John H. Rahe Hughes
1975 Kenneth P.T. Daniels
1983 Richard W. Bateman
1991 Colin Clive Horn

APPENDIX II - CHURCHWARDENS

1609 William Cox
John Raven
1634 James Fremlin
John Gransden
1675 John Gransden
1703 Gregory High
William Round
1721 Thomas Codd
1723 William Pascoe
1726 John Turner
1730 John Haltrop
1735 William Wingate
1767 Richard Kipps
1770-80 Robert Relph
1774 John Turner
1775 Thomas Palmer
1777 John Wigzell
1779 Thomas Taylor
1781 John Bennett
1783 Thomas Kipps
1784-86 Thomas Relph I (P)
1790 John Wigzell (P)
1792 Thomas Taylor
1794 Thomas Bennett
1796 John Turner
1799 Thomas Relph II
1801 John Wigzell
1803 Thomas Taylor
1806 John Turner
1807 John Martin (V)
1809-13 John Bennett (P)
1811 Thomas Relph III
1814-16 Thomas Relph IV
1816 Thomas Bennett

Appendix II - Churchwardens (cont)

1823	William Guest
1843	Thomas Kipps
1843-46	Thomas Burgess
1846-56	George Whitlock
1846	Thomas Bennett
1850-53	Samuel Cheesman
1851-56	John Ray
1853-64	Hezro Holden (V)
1853-62	Samuel Rutley (P)
1865	Thomas Stonham (V)
	Hezro Holden (P)
1863-66	William Hodgson (P)
1865-66	Thomas Stonham (V)
1867-92	Thomas Stonham (P)
1869	No appointment
1870-75	William Rudgard (P)
1876-77	Jabez Larking (P)
1878-81	George Cawston (P)
1882-88	Mark Wilks Collet (P)
1889-98	Sir Mark W. Collet (P)
1893-97	Harry Stonham (V)
1898-03	John Cordery (V)
1899-00	George Hanbury Field (P)
1901-04	Thomas Goldney (P)
1904	John E.C. Bridge (V)
1905-08	Sir Mark E. Collet (P)
1905-11	Thomas Godney (V)
1909-18	Richard Edwards (P)
1912-14	Arthur P. Davison (V)
1915-18	Theophilus Riches (V)
1919	Arthur P. Davison (V)
1919-26	Theophilus Riches (P)
1921-23	William H. Pascoe (V)
1924-36	Capt. William Briggs (V)
1927-28	George Duncan Burnett (P)
1929-31	Edward George Dimon (P)
1932	Capt. Charles N. Boyle (P)
1933-36	George W. Marsh (P)
1937-47	Philip E.C. Burrows (V)
1937-55	Charles J. Pinney (P)
1948-49	J. Geoffrey Bevington (V)
1950-58	Philip E.C. Burrows (V)
1956-62	Victor Ernest Bowden (P)
1959-64	Reginald Charles Ford (V)
1962-65	Edward George Cowlard (P)
1964-80	Thomas Dew (V)
1966-68	Douglas Woodcock (P)
1968-78	Sidney John Payne (P)
1979-80	Michael Bryans (P)
1980-87	Raymond B. Side
1980-	Arthur J.V. Skinner
1987-92	Cyril J. Shrimpton
1992	Ronald Bangay

Appendix III - Lords Of The Manor

1186	William Fitzhelt, Earl of Albermarle
1199	Baldwin de Bethune, Earl of Albermarle
1200	William Marshall, Earl of Pembroke
1208	Fulk de Brent
1216	The Crown (King Henry III)
1231	William Marshall, Earl of Pembroke
1238	Princess Eleanor, Countess of Pembroke
1265	Simon de Montfort, Earl of Leicester
1279	Roger Bigod I, Earl of Norfolk
1283	Roger Bigod II, Earlof Norfolk
1307	Otho de Grandison I
1341	William de Grandison
1347	Peter de Grandison
1360	Otho de Grandison II
1368	Thomas de Grandison
1395	Widow of Thomas de Grandison
1396	Sir William de Bryene
1436	Sir William Fiennes
14--	James Fiennes, Lord Saye and Sele
14--	Sir William Fiennes, Lord Saye and Sele
1463	Sir Geoffrey Bullen
1485	William Bullen
14--	Thomas Bullen, Earl of Wiltshire
15--	George Bullen, Earl of Rochford
1537	The Crown (King Henry VIII)
1541	Queen Anne of Cleves
1558	The Crown (Queen Elizabeth I)
1558	Henry Carey, Lord Hunsdon
1603	John Carey from his brother George, son of Henry
1617	Henry Carey

Thereafter until 1988 the Sackville family of Knole

1988	Anon

APPENDIX IV- CHAIRMEN OF THE PARISH COUNCIL

1894	John Charles Edward Bridge	1936	Gershom Williams
1896	William E. Alexander	1955	Henry Henry
1905	Theophilus Riches	1963	Mrs. Doris Dew
1906	John Goldney	1971	William Roxburgh
1907	Theophilus Riches	1972	Donald A. Eley
1922	Albert Simmons	1977	H. Douglas Kitchener
1925	Captain William Briggs	1987	Anthony M. Davies

APPENDIX V- SEVENOAKS DISTRICT COUNCILLORS

-1957	Walter George Auger	1971-1974	Alan Porter Hunt
1934-1970	Miss Mary Burrows	1973-1987	Godfrey Rollo Croughton
1957-1963	Brigadier H.R.Norman	1987-1991	Donald A. Eley
1963-1966	Phillip Scully	1987-	F.E. Geoffrey Quinn
1966-1987	Mrs Doris Dewer	1991-	Mrs Joyce Course

APPENDIX VI- PARISH CLERKS

1629	William Chowning	1935	Richard Hodder
1654	Nicholas Fremlyn	1945	F. Jarvis
1778	Thomas Golden	1949	Joseph Brewer
1783	William Wynn	1953	Mrs. E.M. Cornford
1802	William Hook	1962	Walter Fenton
1811	John Wickenden	1964	Mrs. Rachel Lawrence
1847	George Kipps	1967	Mrs. Jean Lillicrap
1862	George Kipps	1970	Mrs. Barbara Till
1866	George Kipps	1972	Kenneth Rogers
1894	Alfred George Jordan	1974	Miss W.A. Bloom
1921	A.D. Barham	1978	Mrs. Anne Whitehead
1925	Edgar George Avis	1978	Mrs. Rosemary Banister

APPENDIX VII- SOME CHURCH ORGANISTS

1897	Alexander Marshall	1946	Frank Johnson
1900	John Charles Edward Bridge	1949	Mr. Philpot
1906	Stanley Marchant	1950	Sidney Larcombe
1925	Mr. Hart	1952	Geoffrey Gilbert
1929	Jack Colyer	1953	Stanley R. Smart
1936	Mr. Cowlard	1969	Frank Johnson
1937	Harry Reginald Markham	1991	David Leeke
1941	Mr. Bilham		

APPENDIX VIII- SCHOOL HEADMASTERS

1847	Edward J. Cope	1951	Stanley R. Smart
1885	Albert Bennett	1969	Allan Gilbert
1885	Alfred George Jordan	1985	Paul Hillman
1923	Leonard L. Lowing		

APPENDIX IX- STATION MASTERS

1875-1877	Edwin James Willis	1919	William Knight
1879-1900	Barnaby Barber	1921	Walter Edwin Tapsell
1900	William Nash	1939	Thomas Christopher Foster
1903-1919	William Henry Pettman		

Appendix X- Publicans

THE BELL

1750	John Kipps
1820-21	Mrs Harbour
1841-74	William Jeffrey
1878-93	George Mills
1905	William Colbran
1907	John H. Mills
1916	H.T. Lee
1927	Joe Ames
1936	Mr Gunner
1930-53	Mrs. Martha Ames
1938-39	Arthur Thomas Ames
	Mrs. Muriel Mansfield
1960	Desmond Quinn
1975	Edwin House
1978	
1987	Desmond Marchant

THE WHEATSHEAF

1750	William Elcombe (The Swan)
1839	John Wickham (The Men of Kent)
1847	James Upton
1858	William Geering
1890	Mrs. Sophia Geering
1896	Sidney Joseph Geering
1904	Francis William Wren
1906	Charles Joseph Barnes
1910	William Owen Jarvis Winter
1918	William Henry Small
1948	Thomas Martin
1956	George Charles Hedley
1966	Peter Donald Crisp
1971	Allan Burrows
1986	John Philip Humphrys
1989	Michael Cox

THE CHEQUERS

1828-29	William Wigzell (possibly)
1841-47	Mrs. Sarah Bennett
1851-61	Adam Blackall
1870	Edwin Meades
1874	Henry Briggs
1874	John Woodman
1881	Mrs. Sarah Woodman
1896-1916	George Haseldene
1930	Mrs. Elizabeth Anne Holmden
1930-36	William Kemplen
1936-54	Mrs. Daisy Kemplen
1954-70	Monty Hughes
1970-84	John Burrluck
1984	Barry Draper

Appendix XI- Kemsing Hospital 1914-1918

1028 wounded soldiers were cared for by:-

Commandant: Mrs. Wilkinson (Sister Mabel)

Quartermasters:
Miss Ada C. Waring; Miss Boyle; Mrs. Lacey

VAD Nurses:
Miss I. Davison; Miss M. Fife; Miss E. Goodwin; Miss K. Hobden; Miss D. Hooper; Miss S. Maude; Miss I. Savage; Miss A. Fife; Lady Page Wood; Miss M.C. Gill; Miss N. Goodwin; Miss M. Hodges; Mrs. K. Kingsley; Miss A. Riches; Miss H. Stewart; Miss F.H. Wilkinson.

Trained Nurses:
Sisters Appleyard, Best, Blackwell, D'Arcy, Dibbin, Foster, Clifford, Gill, Goold, Humble, Irwin, Johnson, Kimber, Morral, Percival, Roberts, Ramsley, Scott, Sheehy, Synge, Wallis and Waugh. Mrs. Collier and Mrs. King.

Cooks:
Mrs. J. Jordan, Mrs. May, Mrs. Smithers, Mrs. Woodger, Miss D. Riches, Miss Westmoreland.

Helpers:
Miss Avery, Mrs. Coleridge, Mrs. Hickmott, Mrs. Lingley, Mrs. Mearing, Mrs. Simmons and Miss Williams.

Orderlies:
Pte. Atkinson, Pte. E. Curtis, Pte. Edgar, Pte. Helcy, Pte. Robertson, Pte. G Sellens, Pte. Sheers, Pte. Voulsden and George Wren (civilian).

Appendix XII- Those That Fell In World War I

Harold Avery
George Hicks Bennett
Thomas Boakes
Reginald Pierce Dimon
Thomas Charles Eates
Philip Fenn
Charles William Gunner
Thomas James Holmden
Wilfred Lacey
George Edward Morrison
Harry Nye
William Thomas Read
Arthur Roden
Arthur William Scott
Charles William Scott
Herbert George Skinner
Arthur Slade
Alfred Swaisland
Edward John Vaughan
William Owen Jarvis Winter.

APPENDIXXIII - THOSE WHO FELL IN WORLD WAR II

ROYAL NAVY:

Bushell, Stephen Henry, DSM, CPO - Killed at Hull in an air raid 7.5.41

Newman, Frederick Edward, AB - Killed in action HMS Zinnia, 23.8.41

Hodges, Frank Richard, Ldg Telegraphist - Killed in action HMS Veteran (destroyer) on Atlantic convoy duty August 42.

Hover, Charles William, AB - Killed in action in the Mediterranean,18.11.42

Chitty, Thomas Joseph, AB - Killed at Portsmouth in an air raid 18.6.43, aged 17 1/2 two and a half weeks after volunteering.

Woodgate, Cyril William Thomas, SAB, AA gunner in SS Fort Athabaska, sunk in an air raid on 2.12.43.

Imeson, William John, Stoker 1st class - Died of TB 26.5.44 as a result of war service

THE ARMY:

Hodges, Colin, Spr. RE - Missing presumed killed in France, 19.5.40.

Webster, Maurice, Pte. R. Sussex, - Captured in Belgium 14.6.40 shot as POW 20.9.41.

Davidson, James Edward, Pte. 4 RWK - Missing presumed killed in North Africa 4.9.42.

Thompson, William Henry John, Cpl. 1/7 Queen's - Killed at Alamein 23/24.10.42.

Saturley, Leonard, Pte. 4 Hants - Killed in North Africa, 10.3.43.

Waghorn, Frederick John, Pte. RWK - Killed in North Africa, 30.4.43

Shell, Benjamin Cullen, Pte. 6 RWK - Killed in North Africa, 6.5.43

Kentish, Barbara, Sgt. FANY/WTS - Lost at sea on passage from East Africa to Ceylon (Sri Lanka) 12.2.44

Butler, Henry George, Pte. RWK - Killed in Italy, July 44.

Manktelow, George Walter Philip, Spr. RE - Missing presumed killed in Italy, Sept 44.

Baldwin, Philip Andrew, Pte. RWK - Captured in France 21.5.40 died as a POW 18.2.45

ROYAL AIR FORCE:

Leach, Gerald Charles Somerville, Sgt. - Killed at Benghazi 31.8.41

Turtle, Reginald William Arthur, F/Lt. - Killed on raid on Emden 6.6.42

Hadow, John Maude, F/O - Killed on active service 16.4.43.

APPENDIX XIV - LAND SALES IN 1919

From the map of the sale in July it appears that:-

1. St. Edith's Farm and three cottages were let to Mr. G.M.Davidson.
2. Church Field (i.e. the present Common Field) was sold to Sir Mark Collet for £1,200).
3. West House was let to Mr. A.E. Swaisland for £18 p.a.
4. School Field was let to Mr. Amon Wren.
5. Copperfield and the "window" field opposite the Library were let to Mr. A. E. Swaisland.
6. Noah's Ark Cottage was let to Mr. Amon Wren.
7. The site of Greenlands Road, Fairfield and the east side of Park Lane was farmed by Mr. Amon Wren.
8. Crowdleham House was let to Mr. Marsham.
9. Stonepitts was let to Mr. Philip Symons.
10. Castle Bank was occupied by the Homden, White and Humphrey families.
11. The Keep was occupied by the Meadows and Relf families.
12. Gwen's Cottage was occupied by Mr. Jarvis Winter and Glen Cottage by Mr Haynes.
13. Wybournes Cottages were let to the Slade and Baker families.

From the map of the sale in September it appears that:-

1. There was an oast roundel at each end of Landway Cottages (35-45 West End).
2. The land which is now part of Fairmont, Pilgrims Way, was the "Recreation Field" on which there was a pavilion.
3. One third of Church Field (Common Field) was orchard.
4. There were buildings in the well area.
5. The Post Office was at Clement House and there was a smithy next to it.
6. Five small cottages were attached to Wybournes Cottages (now The Old Forge and New Cottages, High Street).
7. The Box House garden extended northwards to a point opposite Castle Bank.

8. There was a watercress bed at Springhead (now Brookfield) with a building on the west side.
9. Dynes Farm was let to Mr. Thom.
10. Shorehill Farm was let to Mr. W.G. Smith.
11. Cotmans Ash Farm was let to Mr. H. Booker.
12. Heverham Farm was let to Mr. Davidson.
13. Nearly Corner was let to Mr. Edwin Ryder Kipps.
14. Stone Cottages, Heverham, were let to Mr. Clarke and Mr. Pyne.
15. Plum Tree Cottages, Crowdleham, were let to Mr. Davidson.
16. Orchard Cottage, Heverham, was let to Mr. Ewell.
17. The field to the south of Crowdleham Cottage, Cotmans Ash Lane, was let to Miss A.C. Waring.
18. The field opposite Long Downs Cottage was let to Mr. Davidson.
19. The fields round Crowdleham Cottage in Hill Lane (Cotmans Ash Lane) were let to Mr. Davidson.
20. The field opposite Heverham Villas was let to Mr. Davidson.
21. Recreation Field in Five Acre Lane (see No. 2) was let to the Parish Council for £5 p.a.
22. The shop in the High Street (Foster House) was let to Mr. Foster for £27.10s p.a.
23. St. Edith's View was let to the Revd. E.H. Stewart for £13.16s p.a.
24. Rose and Thornton (Well) Cottages were let to Mr. Avery and Mr. Jackson.
25. Dormer Cottage was let to Mr. G. Williams and No. 10 next door to Mr. Thom.
26. Ivy Farm House was let to Mr. May and Ivy Farm Cottage to Mr. A. E. Swaisland.

Appendix XV - Rent Rolls Of Martin & Margery Peckham

Between A.D. 1300 and 1350

1. Roger and Adam, sons and heirs of William de la Hale, gave to the said Martin and Margery and their heirs and assigns three acres of land and three perches with their appurtenances lying at Everhame; towards the west next to the land which was Roger Inkelbold's; towards the east next to the land of Geoffrey Crustel; towards the north next to the land of Laurence Copshed; and towards the south next to the way which leads to the land which belonged to the heir of John Furmager.

2. William Furmager gave to Martin of Peckham one virgate... and a half... helfield... half lies in length to the land of Ralph Furmager towards the east; and the land of Walter Herthey towards the west; and leading to the land which was John de Barmlinges towards the south; and land of the heirs of John Edy to the north. The said virgate indeed lies at Everhame between parkland of Giles Werstin towards the north; and the meadow which was William of Kemsingg's.

3. John Gyles gave to Margery...land...Brodfield in the vill of Kemsyngg next the wood called Dynleahesgrove.

4. Johanne dam of Symon gave to Martin and Margery four acres of land lying in the vill of Kemsyngge between land of Robert of Aldeham towards the west; and a path leading to Makeboltsmed towards the east; and between land of Walter de la Reye and Robert de Aldeham to the north; and land of the heirs of Elianore de Stanepitts south.

5. William the Smith of Everhame gave to Martin and Margery all the meadow which he had at Everhame in a certain meadow called Newmed.

6. The same William (the Smith of Everhame) gave to the same one piece of land lying near Kemesingg at Everhame a field called Suthfield, between land of Giles Warstan towards the E. and W., leading to the land of the said Martin south and the way which leads to the land of the said Giles north. He gave to the same Margery all his share in Dedemede.

7. Reginald son of John Dyn gave...meadow called Fromondsmed in the parish of Kemesyngg as the pales and ditches enclose it.

8. Obsert son of Robert of Aldeham gave to Margery of Peckham all that piece of land which he had in the vill of Kemes in the field called Brodered which was formerly Reg Dyn's.

9. Walter in the Reye gave all that field called Cranstewel lying in Kemesyngg. Paulina and Katharina formerly daughters of Martin de la Sele gave a croft in Kemesyngg lying next to the meadow called Wynterbournemed.

John son of Gyles Warstan gave all the meadow he had in certain meadows called Longmed and Rowemed lying at Keme...Everhame.

Ralph Gyles gave all the mead in Dongemed and Rowemed.

Roger Dyn of La Sele gave seven acres in the field called Brodered.

SOURCES

Information has been taken from many sources, including the following:-

Parish Registers of baptisms, marriages and burials.
Census returns 1841 to 1891
1841 Tithe Apportionment lists
Kelly's Post Office Directories
Dictionary of National Biography
Wills
Archaeologica Cantiana
The Vestry Book
Country Life
Lambeth Palace Library
Notes left by Miss Mary Burrows, Captain A.B. Cross, Mr. Arthur Bailey, and Canon R.V. Bristow
Mr. John Skarratt and his brother Anthony, of Australia.
Mrs. Margaret Stevens

Published references, including:-
William Berry, "Pedigrees of Kent Families, 1830".
G.B. Darbyshire, "Life of St. Edith".
Geoffrey of Monmouth, "History of the Kings of Britain, 1138"
Edward Hasted, "History of Kent, 1778".
John Harris, "History of Kent, 1719".
Sir Charles Igglesden, "A saunter through Kent, 1925".
W.H. Ireland, "History of Kent, 1829".
William Lambarde, "A peregrination of Kent, 1570".
John Leland, "Itinerary of Kent, 1535".
Thomas Philipott, "Villare Cantianum, 1659".
Dr. Gordon Ward, "Sevenoaks Essays".

NOTES FOR FURTHER READING

Kemsing branch library holds the following:-
A Kemsing Chronology - Events year by year since AD 822.
Who was Who in Kemsing - listed alphabetically
Monumental Inscriptions in Kemsing Churchyard - up to1987
House Names in Kemsing.
"All about St. Edith"
"Recollections of My Childhood at Wybournes" by Patricia Douglas.
Kemsing in World War 2
Bound copies of "The Well" (Kemsing Parish Magazine) 1965 to date.

Index

A

B

C

D

E

F

R

S

T

V

W

Y

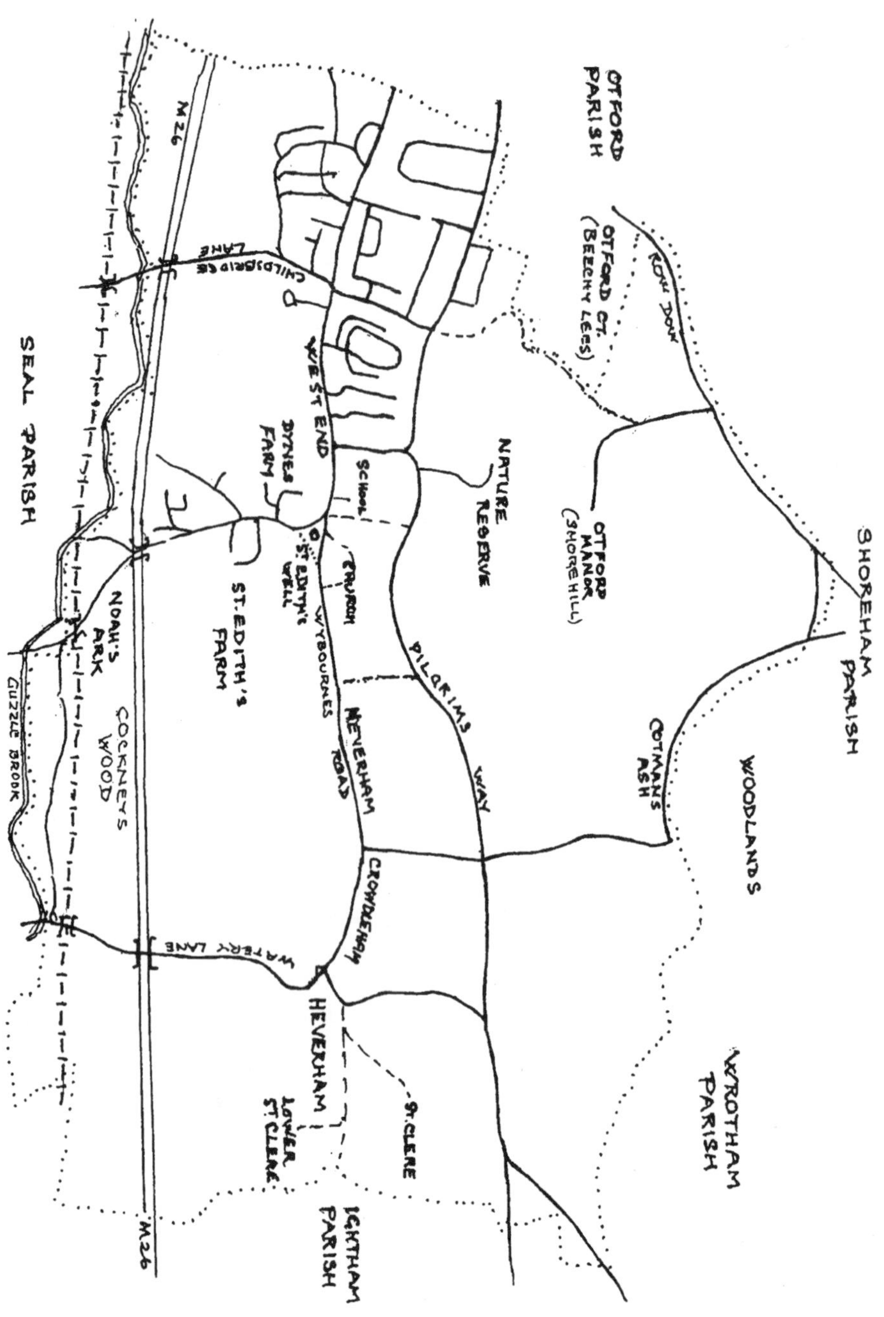
OTFORD PARISH
OTFORD CT. (BEECHY LEES)
ROWDOWN
NATURE RESERVE
OTFORD MANOR (SHOREHILL)
SHOREHAM PARISH
COTMANS ASH
WOODLANDS
WROTHAM PARISH
M26
CHILDSBRIDGE LANE
WEST END
DYNES FARM
SCHOOL
ST EDITH'S WELL
CHURCH
ST. EDITH'S FARM
NOAH'S ARK
WYBOURNES
PILGRIMS WAY
HEVERHAM ROAD
COCKNEYS WOOD
GUZZLE BROOK
SEAL PARISH
CROWDLEHAM
WATERY LANE
HEVERHAM
LOWER ST CLERE
ST. CLERE
IGHTHAM PARISH
M26